SharePoint 2013 Solution Series Volumes 1-10

Volume 1

How To Create a WCF Web Service in SharePoint 2013

STEVEN MANN

How To Create a WCF Web Service in SharePoint 2013

Copyright © 2013 by Steven Mann

Trademarks

Screenshots of Microsoft Products and Services

Warning and Disclaimer

Introduction

Many times you need to access SharePoint data from a web service. This could be for custom web parts, InfoPath Forms, BCS purposes, etc. When you need to access SharePoint data (e.g. list items, document information, etc.), the best method in SharePoint 2013 is to create a custom WCF web service that lives on your SharePoint farm. This Kindle e-book steps you through the process of generating a custom WCF web service that is deployed to SharePoint itself.

Reference links and source code is available on www.stevethemanmann.com:

Step 1 - Visual Studio 2012 Project

The first step is to open up Visual Studio 2012 in a SharePoint development environment and create a new project using the SharePoint Empty Project template:

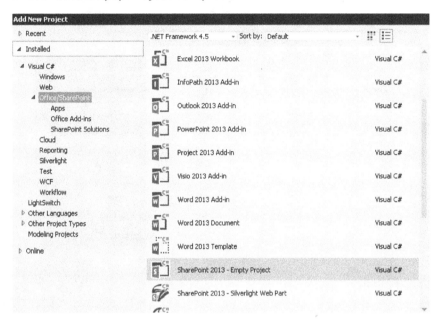

Specify the SharePoint URL for debugging purposes and select Deploy as a farm solution:

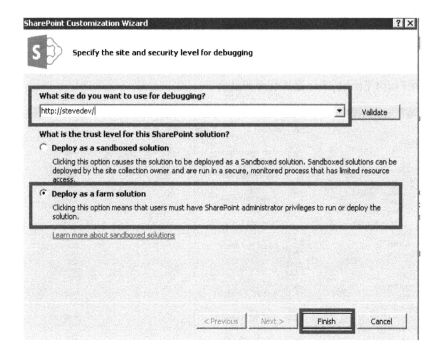

Click Finish.

Step 2 - Leverage the WCF Project Template

Your SharePoint project needs the WCF service components. It is easier to have them generated from a WCF project and copy them into your SharePoint WCF project. Therefore, add a new project to your solution but this time select WCF Service Library:

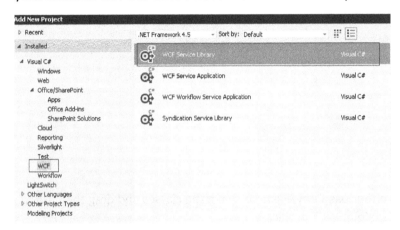

Step 3 - Copy the Service Classes to Your SharePoint WCF Project

Copy the IService1.cs and Service1.cs files that were generated in the WcfServiceLibrary project into your SharePoint WCF project:

You can either use Copy/Paste or select the classes and drag them up to your SharePoint WCF project.

Once these files have been copied into your SharePoint WCF project, you may remove the WCF Service Library project from your solution:

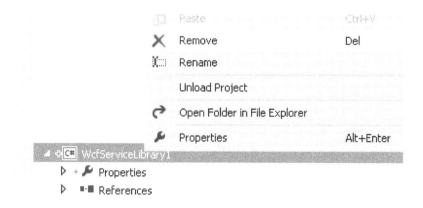

Step 4 - Add References to Your SharePoint WCF Project

You need to add the following references to your SharePoint WCF project:

System.Runtime.Serialization

System.ServiceModel

System.ServiceModel.Web

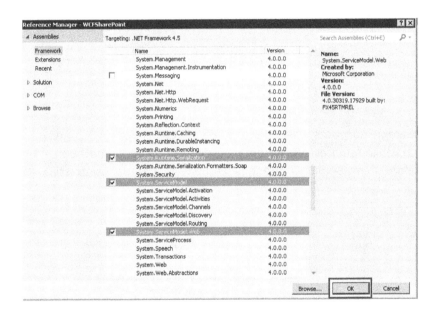

When you create an Empty SharePoint project, the Microsoft.SharePoint and Microsoft.SharePoint.Client.ServerRuntime references are already in place. You no longer need to add these as you may have had done in previous versions of Visual Studio and/or SharePoint.

Step 5 - Define your Service and Data Contracts in the Service Interface

In your interface file (IService1.cs), remove the current operation contracts and define your own for your WCF service.

```
namespace WcfServiceLibrary1
{
    // NOTE: You can use the "Rename" command on the "Refactor" menu to change the in
    [ServiceContract]
    public interface IService1
    {
        [OperationContract]
        string GetData(int value);

        [OperationContract]
        CompositeType GetDataUsingDataContract(CompositeType composite);

        // TODO: Add your service operations here
    }
}
```

For example purposes, I needed to create a WCF Service for BCS and Search which requires a ReadItem method and a ReadList method. Therefore, in my ServiceContract, I created two OperationContracts:

```
[ServiceContract]
public interface IEventsService
{

    [OperationContract]
    EventItem ReadItem(string id);

    [OperationContract]
    List<EventItem> ReadList();

}
```

The implementation of these methods will read list items in a SharePoint Calendar list and return the data within an object. In my example, the object is an EventItem which is a custom class. Therefore, in my DataContract, I needed to define the EventItem class:

```csharp
// Use a data contract as illustrated in the sample bel
[DataContract]
public class EventItem : IComparable, IComparer
{
    private string _eventID;
    [DataMember]
    public string EventID
    {
        get { return _eventID; }
        set { _eventID = value; }
    }


    private string _URL;
    [DataMember]
    public string URL
    {
        get { return _URL; }
        set { _URL = value; }
    }

    private string _title;
    [DataMember]
    public string Title
    {
        get { return _title; }
        set { _title = value; }
    }

    private string _body;
    [DataMember]
    public string Body
    {
        get { return _body; }
        set { _body = value; }
    }
}
```

Notice each property of my class is described as a DataMember
using the [DataMember] attribute.

Step 6 - Prep the Service Class

The service class (Service1.cs) implements the operations that you defined in the interface, however, there are some preparations that need to be performed first.

At the top of the Service1.cs class file, add the following using statements:

using Microsoft.SharePoint;

using Microsoft.SharePoint.Client.Services;

using System.ServiceModel.Activation;

You may copy and paste this from stevethemanmann.com

```
using Microsoft.SharePoint;
using Microsoft.SharePoint.Client.Services;
using System;
using System.Collections.Generic;
using System.Diagnostics;
using System.Linq;
using System.Runtime.Serialization;
using System.ServiceModel;
using System.ServiceModel.Activation;
using System.ServiceModel.Web;
using System.Text;
```

Add the following attributes your service class:

[BasicHttpBindingServiceMetadataExchangeEndpointAttribute]

[AspNetCompatibilityRequirements(RequirementsMode = AspNetCompatibilityRequirementsMode.Required)]

You may copy and paste this from stevethemanmann.com

```
[BasicHttpBindingServiceMetadataExchangeEndpointAttribute]
[AspNetCompatibilityRequirements(RequirementsMode = AspNetCompatibilityRequirementsMode.Required)]
public class EventService : IEventsService
{
```

Step 7 - Implement the Service Methods

In your Service class, add the implementation of the methods that you previously defined within your service interface.

For my BCS example, I needed to implement a ReadItem method:

```
public class EventService : IEventsService
{
    public EventItem ReadItem(string id)
    {
        .....
        return eventItem;
    }
}
```

I also needed to implement a ReadList method:

```
public List<EventItem> ReadList()
{
    List<EventItem> eventItems = new List<EventItem>();
    .....
    return eventItems;
}
```

Step 8 - Create the Share-Point Service Registration File

The moving parts of the WCF service are now completed, however, in order for the service to be deployed and workable in SharePoint, the .svc file needs to be created. The .svc file contains the WCF service information as well as the referenced assembly (.dll) that is generated when you build the solution. The assembly information is added into the registration file upon the build and deployment of your SharePoint WCF Service.

Web services in SharePoint live in the ISAPI folder on each web-front-end and are referenced using /_vti_bin/ within a SharePoint URL. Therefore, you must create an ISAPI folder in your project and then create the registration file within the ISAPI folder.

Right-click your SharePoint WCF project and select Add. Then select SharePoint Mapped folder...

The Add SharePoint Mapped Folder dialog appears.

In the Add SharePoint Mapped Folder dialog select ISAPI and click OK:

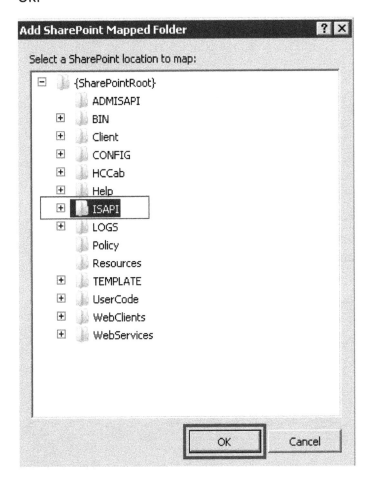

The ISAPI folder is added to your project.

Next, you need to create the registration file within the ISAPI folder. Therefore, right-click the ISAPI folder in your project and select Add. Select New Item...

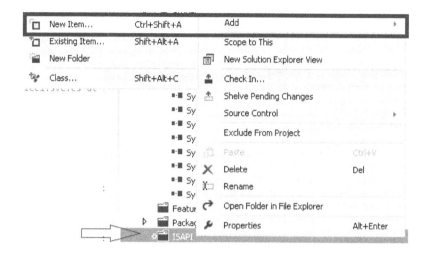

From the General section, select Text File and name your file with a .svc extension. Click Add:

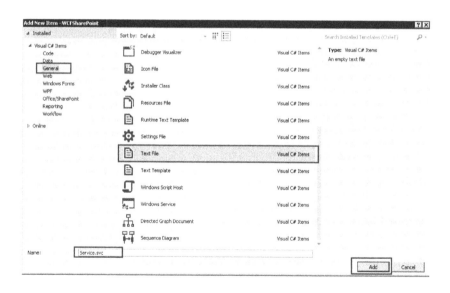

Open the Service.svc file that was created and add the following code:

```
<%@ServiceHost Language="C#" Debug="true"
   Service="WcfService.ServiceName, $SharePoint.Project.AssemblyFullName$"
   Facto-
ry="Microsoft.SharePoint.Client.Services.MultipleBaseAddressBasicHttpBindingSe
rviceHostFactory, Microsoft.SharePoint.Client.ServerRuntime, Version=15.0.0.0,
Culture=neutral,
PublicKeyToken=71e9bce111e9429c" %>
```

You may copy and paste this from stevethemanmann.com

Save the file changes.

Step 9 - Activate Token Replacements for Service Files

The code that you pasted into the .svc file contains the assembly full name token ($SharePoint.Project.AssemblyFullName$). Visual Studio replaces this with the assembly from your project during build and deployment. However, you must instruct Visual Studio to perform this in .svc files.

This requires a modification to the actual project file of your SharePoint WCF service. Since it is open in Visual Studio, first right-click your project and select Unload Project.

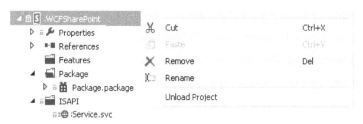

Now locate the project file from the file system and edit in a text editor (e.g. NotePad).

Add the following property tag to the project file within the <PropertyGroup> section:

<TokenReplacementFileExtensions>svc</TokenReplacementFileExtensions>

```
_                  WCFSharePoint - Notepad                                                                          _ □ X
File  Edit  Format  View  Help
<?xml version="1.0" encoding="utf-8"?>
<Project Toolsversion="4.0" DefaultTargets="Build" xmlns="http://schemas.microsoft.com/developer/msbuild/2003">
  <Import Project="$(MSBuildExtensionsPath)\$(MSBuildToolsVersion)\Microsoft.Common.props" Condition="Exists('$(MSBuildExten
  <PropertyGroup>
    <Configuration Condition=" '$(Configuration)' == '' ">Debug</Configuration>
    <Platform Condition=" '$(Platform)' == '' ">AnyCPU</Platform>
    <ProjectGuid>{3F899188-A0B6-4B5B-8087-8087-9E6F1FC4B7E1}</ProjectGuid>
    <OutputType>Library</OutputType>
    <AppDesignerFolder>Properties</AppDesignerFolder>
    <RootNamespace>FirmEventsWCFSharePoint</RootNamespace>
    <AssemblyName>FirmEventsWCFSharePoint</AssemblyName>
    <TargetFrameworkVersion>v4.5</TargetFrameworkVersion>
    <Targetofficeversion>15.0</Targetofficeversion>
    <FileAlignment>512</FileAlignment>
    <ProjectTypeGuids>{C1CDDADD-2546-481F-9697-4EA41081F2FC};{14822709-B5A1-4724-98CA-57A101D1B079};{FAE04EC0-301F-11D3-BF4B
    <SccProjectName>SAK</SccProjectName>
    <SccLocalPath>SAK</SccLocalPath>
    <SccAuxPath>SAK</SccAuxPath>
    <SccProvider>SAK</SccProvider>
    <TokenReplacementFileExtensions>svc</TokenReplacementFileExtensions>|
  </PropertyGroup>
  <PropertyGroup Condition=" '$(Configuration)|$(Platform)' == 'Debug|AnyCPU' ">
    <DebugSymbols>true</DebugSymbols>
    <DebugType>full</DebugType>
    <Optimize>false</Optimize>
    <OutputPath>bin\Debug\</OutputPath>
    <DefineConstants>DEBUG;TRACE</DefineConstants>
    <ErrorReport>prompt</ErrorReport>
    <WarningLevel>4</WarningLevel>
    <UseVSHostingProcess>false</UseVSHostingProcess>
  </PropertyGroup>
  <PropertyGroup Condition=" '$(Configuration)|$(Platform)' == 'Release|AnyCPU' ">
    <DebugType>pdbonly</DebugType>
    <Optimize>true</Optimize>
    <OutputPath>bin\Release\</OutputPath>
```

Save the changes and Reload the project within Visual Studio:

Step 10 - Deploy Your SharePoint WCF Service

Right-click your solution and select Deploy. Visual Studio builds your solution, generates an assembly, updates the .svc file, creates a WSP file for deployment to stage/production, and deploys your SharePoint WCF service to your development SharePoint environment.

Step 11 - Test Your Share-Point WCF in SharePoint

Once your solution has been deployed, you may access the WCF service in SharePoint using the SharePoint root URL along with the path to the service:

http://<<sharepoint root>>/_vti_bin/Service.svc

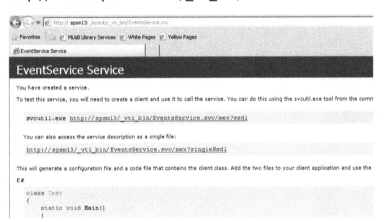

To fully test the service you need to call it from a client application or use the svcutil.exe tool to invoke the service methods to insure data is being returned.

Using Your WCF Service in BCS

When creating an external content type using a SharePoint WCF Service, you need to enter and select the proper selections. This section shows examples of these settings:

Service Metadata URL

http://<<sharepoint root>/_vti_bin/Service.svc/mex?wsdl

Metadata Connection Mode

WSDL

Service EndPoint URL

http://<<sharepoint root>>/_vti_bin/Service.svc

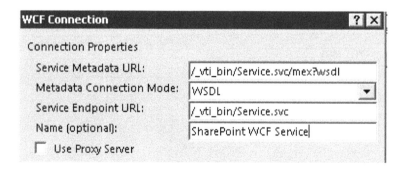

Conclusion

In just a handful of steps you can easily create a WCF Service in SharePoint that serves up SharePoint data. Using the WCF Service Library template as a guide and an empty SharePoint project, Visual Studio 2012 provides the tools and functionality to generate and deploy a SharePoint WCF service.

I hope you found this guide useful and informative. If you have any troubles or other questions, please send them to me at steve@stevethemanmann.com.

Volume 2

How To Integrate BCS with Search in SharePoint 2013

STEVEN MANN

How To Integrate BCS with Search in SharePoint 2013

Copyright © 2013 by Steven Mann

Trademarks

Screenshots of Microsoft Products and Services

Warning and Disclaimer

Introduction

This guide steps you through the process of incorporating external data into SharePoint 2013 Search by leveraging Business Data Connectivity Services (BCS). It provides an end-to-end solution that integrates product data from a SQL Server database into SharePoint by using external content types. Creating a new search vertical as well as customizing the display and hover panels of the business data search results is also covered.

Reference links and source code are available on www.stevethemanmann.com:

Step 1: Prepare the Data Source

The scenario and sample data for this guide uses Product information from the

AdventureWorks2012 sample database in SQL Server.

The first step is to create your read list and read item procedures.

Create a stored procedure that returns all of the information you want to search and make sure all rows are returned:

```
CREATE PROCEDURE GetAllProductsForWCS
AS
BEGIN
    -- SET NOCOUNT ON added to prevent extra result sets from
       interfering with SELECT statements.
    SET NOCOUNT ON;

    -- Insert statements for procedure here
    SELECT
        p.ProductID,
        p.ProductNumber,
        p.Name AS ProductName,
        p.Class AS ProductClass,
        p.Color AS ProductColor,
        p.ProductLine,
        p.ListPrice AS ProductListPrice,
        pc.Name AS ProductCategory,
        psc.Name AS ProductSubCategory,
        pm.Name AS ProductModel,
        pd.Description as ProductDescription
    FROM Production.Product p
```

	ProductID	ProductNumber	ProductName	ProductClass	ProductColor	ProductLine	ProductListPrice	ProductCategory	ProductSubCategory	ProductModel	ProductDescription
1	994	BB-7421	LL Bottom Bracket	L	NULL	NULL	53.99	Components	Bottom Brackets	LL Bottom Bracket	Chromoly steel.
2	995	BB-8107	ML Bottom Bracket	M	NULL	NULL	101.24	Components	Bottom Brackets	ML Bottom Bracket	Aluminum alloy cups; large d
3	996	BB-9108	HL Bottom Bracket	H	NULL	NULL	121.49	Components	Bottom Brackets	HL Bottom Bracket	Aluminum alloy cups and a h
4	984	BK-M18S-40	Mountain-500 Silver, 40	L	Silver	M	564.99	Bikes	Mountain Bikes	Mountain-500	Suitable for any type of riding
5	985	BK-M18S-42	Mountain-500 Silver, 42	L	Silver	M	564.99	Bikes	Mountain Bikes	Mountain-500	Suitable for any type of riding
6	986	BK-M18S-44	Mountain-500 Silver, 44	L	Silver	M	564.99	Bikes	Mountain Bikes	Mountain-500	Suitable for any type of riding
7	987	BK-M18S-48	Mountain-500 Silver, 48	L	Silver	M	564.99	Bikes	Mountain Bikes	Mountain-500	Suitable for any type of riding
8	988	BK-M18S-52	Mountain-500 Silver, 52	L	Silver	M	564.99	Bikes	Mountain Bikes	Mountain-500	Suitable for any type of riding
9	989	BK-M18B-40	Mountain-500 Black, 40	L	Black	M	539.99	Bikes	Mountain Bikes	Mountain-500	Suitable for any type of riding
10	990	BK-M18B-42	Mountain-500 Black, 42	L	Black	M	539.99	Bikes	Mountain Bikes	Mountain-500	Suitable for any type of riding
11	991	BK-M18B-44	Mountain-500 Black, 44	L	Black	M	539.99	Bikes	Mountain Bikes	Mountain-500	Suitable for any type of riding
12	992	BK-M18B-48	Mountain-500 Black, 48	L	Black	M	539.99	Bikes	Mountain Bikes	Mountain-500	Suitable for any type of riding
13	993	BK-M18B-52	Mountain-500 Black, 52	L	Black	M	539.99	Bikes	Mountain Bikes	Mountain-500	Suitable for any type of riding
14	980	BK-M38S-38	Mountain-400-W Silver, 38	M	Silver	M	769.49	Bikes	Mountain Bikes	Mountain-400-W	This bike delivers a high leve

I created a GetAllProductsForBCS stored procedure which returns the product information I need using several joins:

```
CREATE PROCEDURE GetAllProductsForBCS
AS
BEGIN
        -- SET NOCOUNT ON added to prevent extra result sets
from
        -- interfering with SELECT statements.
        SET NOCOUNT ON;

    -- Insert statements for procedure here
        SELECT
                p.ProductID,
                p.ProductNumber,
                p.Name AS ProductName,
                p.Class AS ProductClass,
                p.Color AS ProductColor,
                p.ProductLine,
                p.ListPrice AS ProductListPrice,
                pc.Name AS ProductCategory,
                psc.Name AS ProductSubCategory,
                pm.Name AS ProductModel,
                pd.Description as ProductDescription
        FROM Production.Product p
                INNER JOIN Production.ProductSubcategory psc
                    ON psc.ProductSubcategoryID =
p.ProductSubcategoryID
                INNER JOIN Production.ProductCategory pc
                    ON pc.ProductCategoryID =
psc.ProductCategoryID
                INNER JOIN Production.ProductModel pm
                    on pm.ProductModelID = p.ProductModelID
                INNER JOIN Produc-
tion.ProductModelProductDescriptionCulture pmx
                    ON pm.ProductModelID = pmx.ProductModelID
                INNER JOIN Production.ProductDescription pd
                    ON pmx.ProductDescriptionID =
pd.ProductDescriptionID
        WHERE pmx.CultureID='en'
```

This procedure is used to create a ReadList method in the External Content Type.

Create a stored procedure that returns the same information but only for a particular entity by using the ID as a parameter:

```sql
-- ===== GetProductByProductIDForDLS 995
CREATE PROCEDURE GetProductByProductIDForDLS (@ProductID INT)
AS
BEGIN
    -- SET NOCOUNT ON added to prevent extra result sets from
    -- interfering with SELECT statements.
    SET NOCOUNT ON;

    -- Insert statements for procedure here
    SELECT
        p.ProductID,
        p.ProductNumber,
        p.Name AS ProductName,
        p.Class AS ProductClass,
        p.Color AS ProductColor,
        p.ProductLine,
        p.ListPrice AS ProductListPrice,
        pc.Name AS ProductCategory,
        psc.Name AS ProductSubCategory,
        pm.Name AS ProductModel,
        pd.Description as ProductDescription
    FROM Production.Product p
        INNER JOIN Production.ProductSubcategory psc
            ON psc.ProductSubcategoryID = p.ProductSubcategoryID
        INNER JOIN Production.ProductCategory pc
            ON pc.ProductCategoryID = psc.ProductCategoryID
        INNER JOIN Production.ProductModel pm
            on pm.ProductModelID = p.ProductModelID
        INNER JOIN Production.ProductModelProductDescriptionCulture pmx
            ON pm.ProductModelID = pmx.ProductModelID
        INNER JOIN Production.ProductDescription pd
            ON pmx.ProductDescriptionID = pd.ProductDescriptionID
    WHERE p.ProductID = @ProductID
        AND pmx.CultureID='en'
```

ProductID	ProductNumber	ProductName	ProductClass	ProductColor	ProductLine	ProductListPrice	ProductCategory	ProductSubCategory	ProductModel	ProductDescription
1	995	BB-9107	ML Bottom Bracket	M	NULL	NULL	101.24	Components	Bottom Brackets	ML Bottom Bracket	Aluminum alloy cups; large diameter

Make sure only 1 row is returned for a given identity.

I created a GetAllProductsForBCS stored procedure which returns the product information I need based on the passed in ProductID parameter:

```
CREATE PROCEDURE GetProductByProductIDForBCS (@ProductID INT)
AS
BEGIN
        -- SET NOCOUNT ON added to prevent extra result sets
from
        -- interfering with SELECT statements.
        SET NOCOUNT ON;

    -- Insert statements for procedure here
        SELECT
                p.ProductID,
                p.ProductNumber,
                p.Name AS ProductName,
                p.Class AS ProductClass,
                p.Color AS ProductColor,
                p.ProductLine,
                p.ListPrice AS ProductListPrice,
                pc.Name AS ProductCategory,
                psc.Name AS ProductSubCategory,
                pm.Name AS ProductModel,
                pd.Description as ProductDescription
        FROM Production.Product p
                INNER JOIN Production.ProductSubcategory psc
                        ON psc.ProductSubcategoryID =
p.ProductSubcategoryID
                INNER JOIN Production.ProductCategory pc
                        ON pc.ProductCategoryID =
psc.ProductCategoryID
                INNER JOIN Production.ProductModel pm
                        on pm.ProductModelID = p.ProductModelID
                INNER JOIN Produc-
tion.ProductModelProductDescriptionCulture pmx
                        ON pm.ProductModelID = pmx.ProductModelID
                INNER JOIN Production.ProductDescription pd
                        ON pmx.ProductDescriptionID =
pd.ProductDescriptionID
        WHERE p.ProductID = @ProductID
                AND pmx.CultureID='en'
```

This procedure is used to create a ReadItem method in the External Content Type. The SELECT statement here should be exactly the same as the SELECT in the ReadList. The only difference here is that additional WHERE condition for the passed in @ProductID.

Step 2: Add Credentials to the Secure Store Service

In order for the External Content Type to be created and BCS to access your external data source, the data source credentials need to be stored. The Secure Store Service in SharePoint allows you to store credentials. For this scenario, a SQL database account was created named "AWDBAccount". Therefore an entry in the Secure Store Service needs to be added for SQL Authentication.

Navigate to Central Administration and click on Manage Service Applications under the Application Management section:

Click on the Secure Store Service application link:

If you do not have a Secure Store Service listed, you'll need to create one.

If you see a message at the top of the screen regarding a key, click the Generate New Key button from the top ribbon:

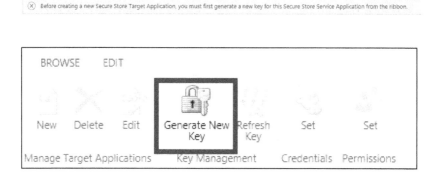

Enter a pass phrase and click OK:

Click New from the top ribbon:

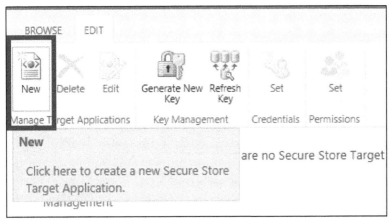

Enter a Target Application ID, Display Name, and Contact E-mail:

You will need the Target Application ID to create the External Content Type. Click Next.

Change the Windows User Name field name to User ID the Windows Password field name to Password.

Change the associated Field Types from to User Name and Password. Click Next.

Enter Target Application Administrators and click OK:

The Target Application entry is created:

Select the Target Application checkbox and click the Set Credentials button:

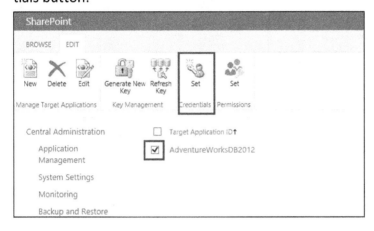

Enter the Credential Owner (this should be the service account that runs BCS), enter the SQL database User ID and Password. Click OK:

Step 3: Create an External Content Type

The methods here describe the steps for a no-code solution in creating an External Content Type that uses your data source as the provider of information via SharePoint Designer 2013.

Launch SharePoint Designer 2013 and open your Search Center site:

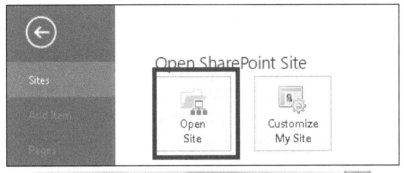

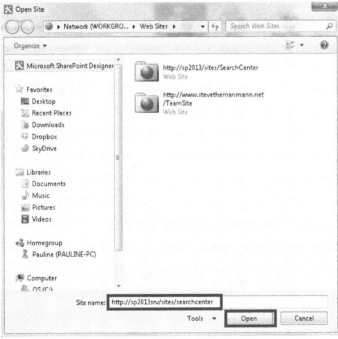

Click the External Content Types from the Site Objects and then click the External Content Type button from the top-ribbon:

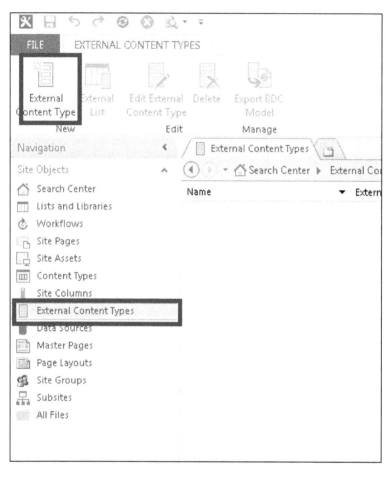

Enter a Name and Display Name and then click on the External System link:

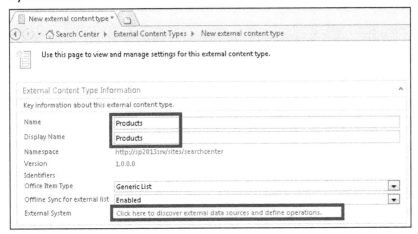

Click on the Add Connection button:

Select the type of connection. For this example, SQL Server is be-ing used:

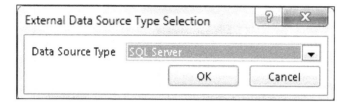

Click OK.

Enter the Database Server, the Database Name, and select Con-nect with Impersonated Custom Identity. Enter the Secure Store Application ID that was created in the previous section:

SQL Server Connection

Connection Properties

Database Server: SQLSRV2012

Database Name: AdventureWorks2012

Name (optional): Adventure Works 2012

○ Connect with User's Identity

○ Connect with Impersonated Windows Identity

◉ Connect with Impersonated Custom Identity

Secure Store Application ID: AdventureWorksDB2012

OK   Cancel

Click OK.

If prompted, enter SQL Server credentials to access the database.

Expand the database in the Data Source Explorer tab and then expand the Routines folder. Locate the Read List procedure, right click and select New Read List Operation:

Enter an Operation Name and Display Name.

The Operation Name becomes a prefix (ReadList.propertyname) in the crawled properties so it is a good idea to include an entity description in the name, otherwise it would be hard to distinguish crawled properties from their external content types.

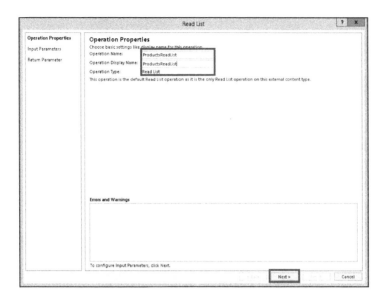

Click Next.

The example does not limit the Read List items and thus there are no Input Parameters. Click Next:

On the Return Parameter Configuration screen, make sure the row identifier (primary key) is selected and check the Map to

Identifier checkbox. The Identifier, Field, and DisplayName become populated with the row identifier. Click Finish.

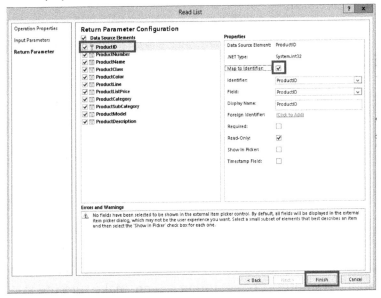

Next, locate the Read Item procedure, right click and select New Read Item Operation:

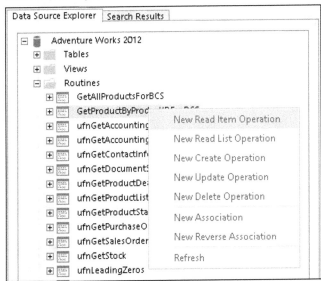

Enter appropriate operation names. Click Next:

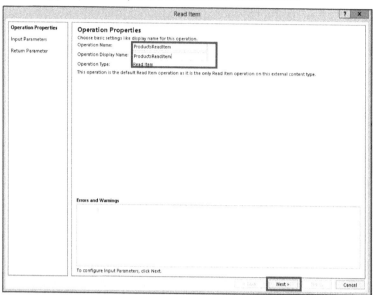

On the Input Parameters Configuration screen, make sure the input parameter is selected and the Map to Identifier is checked. Click Next:

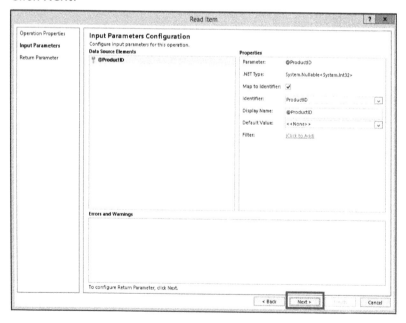

On the Return Parameter Configuration screen, make sure the row identifier (primary key) is selected and check the Map to

Identifier checkbox. The Identifier, Field, and DisplayName become populated with the row identifier. Click Finish.

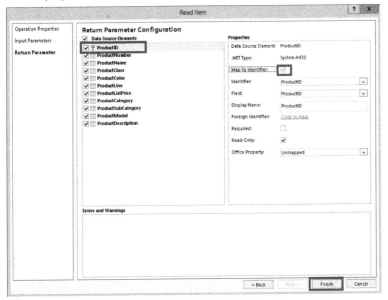

The new operations appear in the External Content Type Operations section:

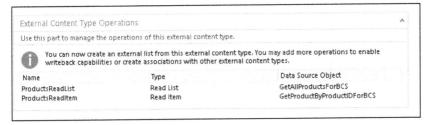

Save the External Content Type:

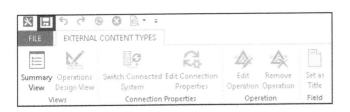

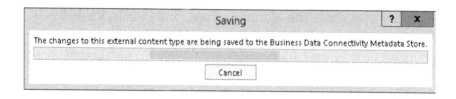

Keep SharePoint Designer 2013 open to the External Content Type. Navigate to your Business Data Connectivity Service Application and verify the new external content type exists:

In your Business Data Connectivity Service Application, click the Configure button.

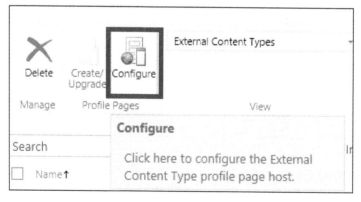

Enter a location to host the External Content Type profile pages:

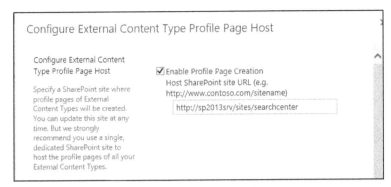

It is recommended to use a dedicate SharePoint site. I personally like things being all together in my Search Center Site Collection so I use that.

Scroll down and click OK.

While you are here you could set the permissions in the BCS for the External Content type as explained in the next section (or just come back to it).

Navigate back to SharePoint Designer 2013 and with the External Content Type opened, click on the Create Profile Page button from the top-ribbon:

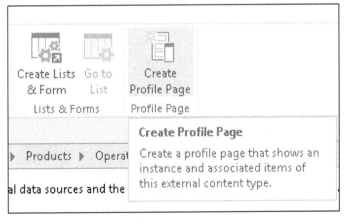

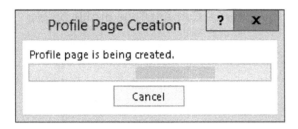

The Profile Page is created. This page becomes used for the search results URL if a custom URL (page) is not used as part of the data source.

Step 4: Set Permissions on the BCS Entity

Navigate to your Business Data Connectivity Service Application and select the External Content Type by checking the checkbox:

Click on the Set Object Permissions button from the top-ribbon.

Enter accounts into the account box (if your external content type is for general use include Everyone):

Click Add. Select each added account and check off the appropriate permissions. For Everyone, only check off Execute and Selectable In Clients.

Click OK.

Step 5: Create a Content Source for the External Content Type

Navigate to Central Administration and click on Manage service applications:

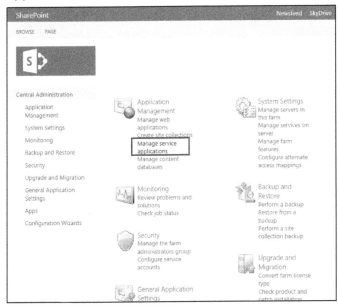

Click on the Search Service Application:

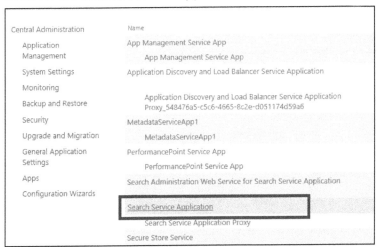

Click on Content Sources under Crawling (in the left hand column):

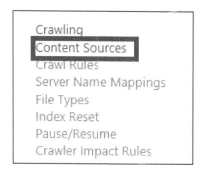

On the Manage Content Source page click the New Content Source link:

Enter a name for the Content Source and select Line of Business Data. Select the Crawl selected external data source and check off the data source:

Scroll down and click OK.

The content source is created and listed on the Manage Content Sources page:

Hover over the new content source and click the drop-down menu. Select Start Full Crawl:

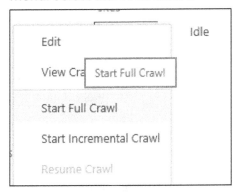

Step 6: Create Managed Properties Based on Crawled Properties

After the crawl has completed, you now need to create managed properties and map them to the crawled properties from the new content source. This may be accomplished from the Search Service Application UI or from PowerShell. Either way, you need to know what crawled properties have been created.

From the Search Service Application, click on Search Schema on the left hand side of the screen under Queries and Results:

On the Managed Properties page, click on Crawled Properties at the top:

Select Business Data from the Category drop-down and click the
filter button:

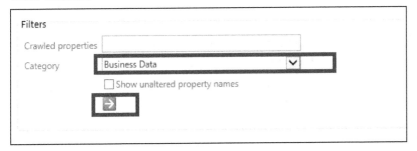

The crawled properties from the external data source are displayed:

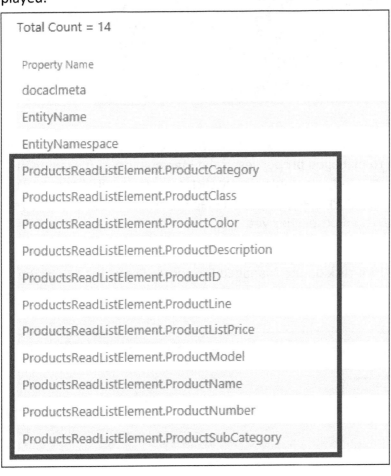

You may also use PowerShell to list out the crawled properties. I use the following commands:

Add-PSSnapin Microsoft.SharePoint.PowerShell -ErrorAction SilentlyContinue

$ssa = Get-SPEnterpriseSearchServiceApplication

Get-SPEnterpriseSearchMetadataCrawledProperty -SearchApplication $ssa -Category 'Business Data' | ft Name

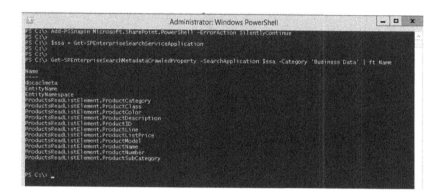

Now that you know what the crawled properties are, you can map them to managed properties. If the managed properties were already created, you could simply click on each crawled property on the Crawled Property page and map them. In this case, there are no managed properties yet.

Therefore click on the Managed Properties link at the top of the Crawled Properties page:

On the Managed Properties page, click on New Managed Property:

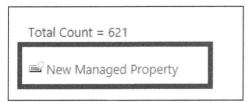

Enter a name for the property. I usually prefix them with the entity type so they are all displayed together and I know which content source they are from. Select the Type and check the Searchable checkbox:

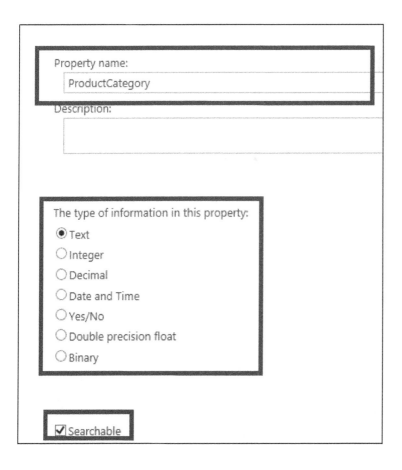

Scroll down and check Queryable and Retrievable. For this example, the Product Category will be refinable and sortable so I selected "Yes -active" for both of those entries:

For external content I usually select Include content from the first crawled property setting. These should be one-to-one mappings so it really doesn't make a difference. Click on the Add Mapping button:

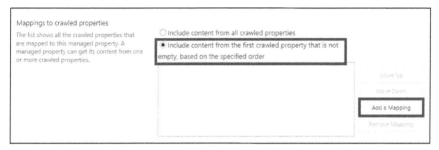

In the Crawled property dialog, select Business Data from the filter drop-down. Select the appropriate crawled property and click OK.

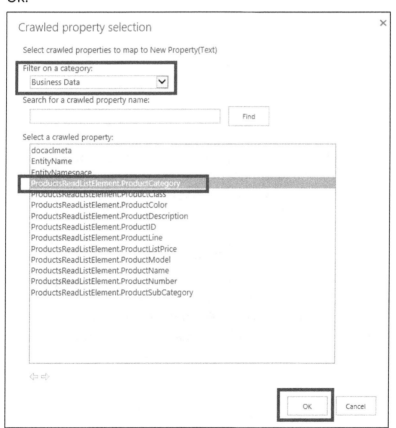

Back on the Add Managed Property page, click OK:

You'll need to repeat this process for each crawled property.

Performing the mapping through the UI can become tedious. That's why I create a script to map all of my properties:

```
Add-PSSnapin Microsoft.SharePoint.PowerShell -ErrorAction SilentlyContinue
$ssa = Get-SPEnterpriseSearchServiceApplication

$crawledProperty = Get-SPEnterpriseSearchMetadataCrawledProperty -SearchApplication $ssa -Name ProductsReadListElement.ProductCategory
$managedProperty = New-SPEnterpriseSearchMetadataManagedProperty -SearchApplication $ssa -Name ProductCategory -FullTextQueriable:$true -Queryable:$true -Retrievable:$true -Type 1
New-SPEnterpriseSearchMetadataMapping -SearchApplication $ssa -ManagedProperty $managedProperty -CrawledProperty $crawledProperty
```

Just repeat the last three lines for each property mapping.

There are no parameters for sortable or refinable so I just go into the UI and change those settings manually for the properties I want to sort on or refine. You could create the crawled property if you knew what it was going to be named but in my script I get the crawled property since it was already created.

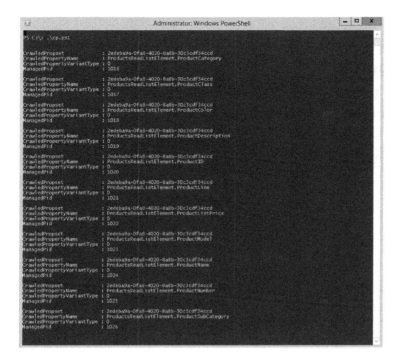

In order for the Managed Properties to take effect, you now need to run a full crawl on the content source again.

Step 7: Create a Result Source for the New Content Source

Navigate to your Search Center and select Site Settings from the Settings menu:

Under the Site Collection Administration section, click on Search Result Sources:

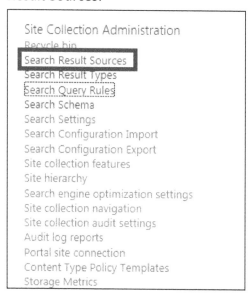

On the Manage Result Sources page, click on the New Result Source link:

On the Add Result Source page, enter a name for the Result Source. For this example, I am using Products:

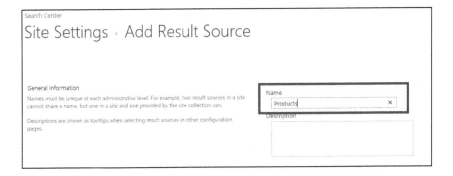

Scroll down and click on the Launch Query Builder button:

In the Property Filter section, first select "--Show all managed properties--":

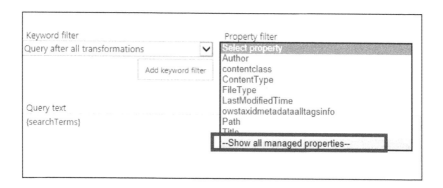

Next select ContentSource from the drop-down. Select Equals and Manual value:

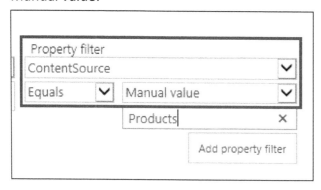

Enter the name of the content source (e.g. Products) in the text box and click Add property filter:

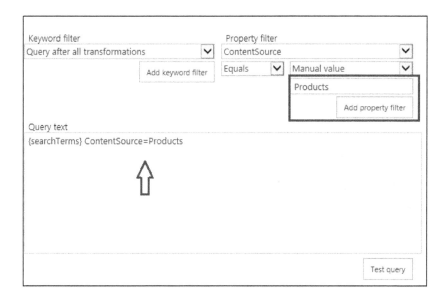

The property filter is added to the Query text.

Click OK on the Build Your Query dialog. The property filter is added to the Query Transform text box.

Click Save:

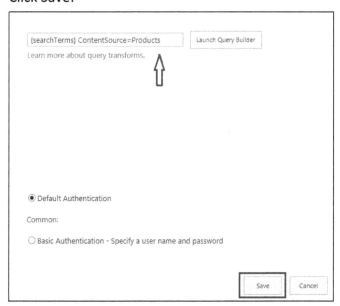

The new result source is created and appears under the Defined for this site section:

Site Collection Administration

Use result sources to scope search results and federate queries to exter

Result Sources replace Search Scopes, which are now deprecated. You

🖳 New Result Source

Name

Defined for this site collection (1)

Products

Provided by SharePoint (16)

Step 8: Create a Result Type for the Result Source

Navigate to your Search Center and select Site Settings from the Settings menu.

Under the Site Collection Administration section, click on the Search Result Types link:

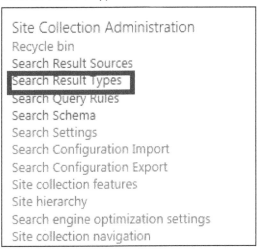

On the Result Types page click on the New Result Type link:

Enter a name for the Result Type. Select the Result Source created in the previous section from the source drop-down. Skip the types of content rule. Select Default Item for now under "What should these results look like?". You will create a custom item template in later sections.

Site Collection Administration › Add Result Type

apply to all sites in the site collection. To make one for just this site, use site result types.

Give it a name

> Products

Which source should results match?

> Products ▾

What types of content should match? You can skip this rule to match all content

> Select a value ▾

Add value

What should these results look like?

> Default Item ▾

Note: This result type will automatically update with the latest properties in your display template each time you visit the Manage Result Types Page.

Display template URL

~sitecollection/_catalogs/masterpage/Display Templates/Search/Item_Default.js

☐ Optimize for frequent use

Save   Cancel

Click Save.

Step 9: Create a Search Results Page for the New Content Source

Navigate to your Search Center and select Site Contents from the Settings menu:

Locate and double-click the Pages library:

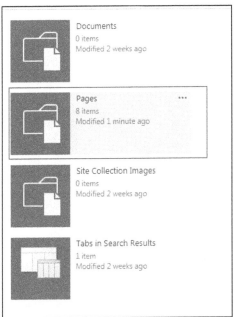

From the Files tab in the top ribbon, select Page from the New Document drop-down menu:

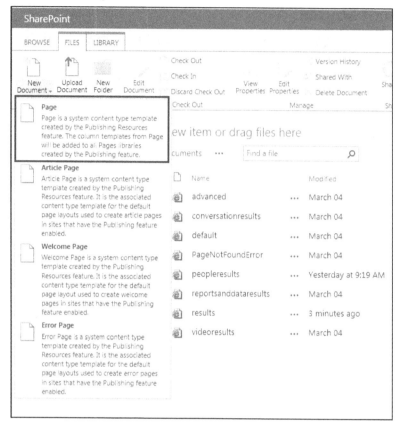

On the Create Page page, enter a title and URL Name. Click Create.

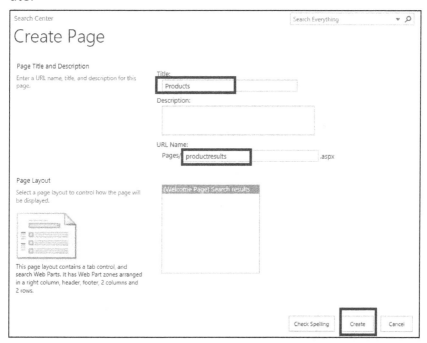

Select the ellipsis menu on the new page and click on OPEN:

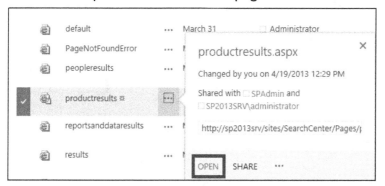

From the Settings menu select Edit page:

Locate the Search Results web part and select Edit Web Part from the drop-down menu:

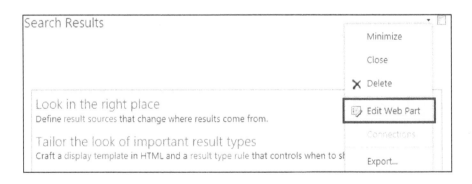

In the Properties tool pane that appeared on the right, click the Change query button:

The Build Your Query dialog appears.

In the Select a query section, select the custom Result Source created in the previous section of this chapter:

Click OK on the Build Your Query dialog.

Click OK in the web part properties tool pane:

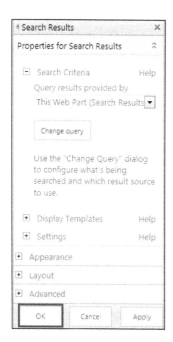

Check in the page. Publish the page.

Step 10: Add a Custom Results Page to the Search Center Navigation

Navigate to your Search Center and select Site Settings from the Settings menu:

Under the Search section click the Search Settings link:

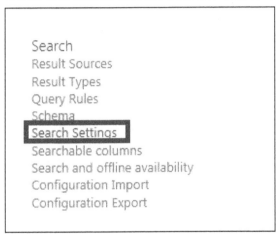

At the bottom the Search Settings page, click on Add Link…:

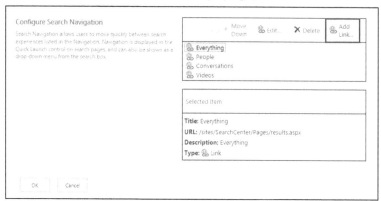

Enter a title and the URL to the custom page that was created in the previous section. Click OK.

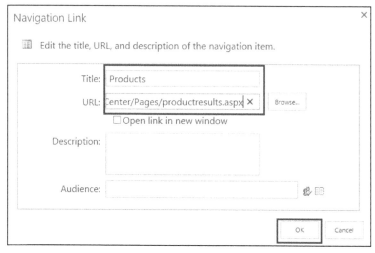

Back on the Search Settings page click OK:

Step 11: Test the Results

Navigate to your Search Center. The new navigation item appears at the top. Click on the new link and perform a search:

The results aren't too pretty. The next section explains how to create custom item templates and hover panels for the external content source.

Step 12: Create an Item Display Template

Fire up SharePoint Designer 2013 and Open the Search Center Site:

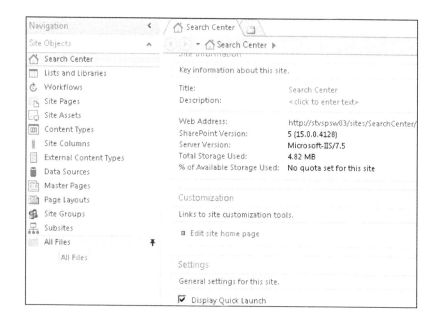

Click on All Files from the left-hand navigation:

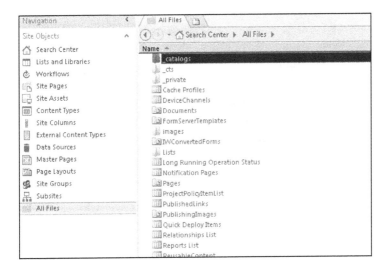

A list of all files is displayed in the main window.

If you attempt to get the files from the Master Pages object, you will not see any items once you get to the Display Templates folders.

Double-click on the _catalogs folder in the main window
This action displays the _catalogs structure under the left-hand
navigation.

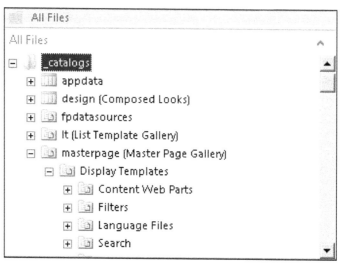

Expand the _catalogs folder, then the masterpage folder, and
then the Display Templates folder.

Click on the Search folder under Display Templates:

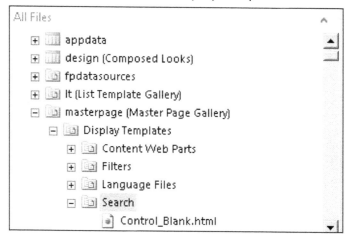

The list of Search display templates is shown in the main window
area.

Locate Item_Default.html and Item_Default.js. Select both files, right-click, and select copy:

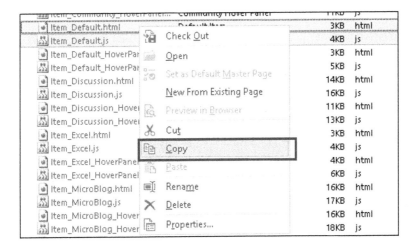

Right click again and select Paste:

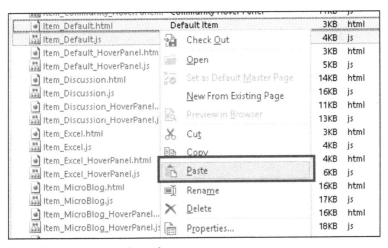

The files are copied in place.

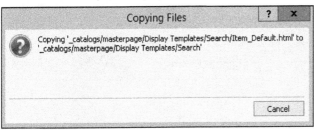

Rename the html copy:

Item_Default.html	Default Item
Item_Default.js	Default Item
Item_Product.html	Default Item
Item_Default_copy(1).js	Default Item
Item_Default_HoverPanel.html	Default Hover Panel
Item_Default_HoverPanel.js	Default Hover Panel

SharePoint automatically renames the .js file:

Item_PowerPoint_HoverPane...	PowerPoint Hover Panel	10KB	js
Item_Product.html	Default Item	3KB	html
Item_Product.js	Default Item	4KB	js
Item_Reply.html	Reply Item	14KB	html
Item_Reply.js	Reply Item	15KB	js

Right-click the html file and select Edit File in Advanced Mode:

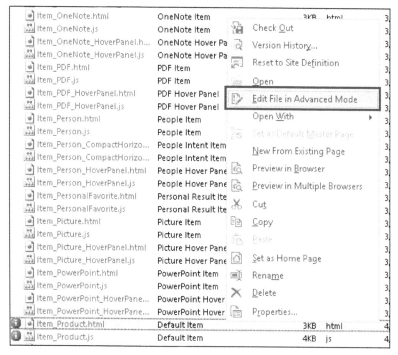

Rename the title:

```
1  <html xmlns:mso="urn:schemas-microsoft-com:office:office" xmlns:
2  <head>
3  <title>Product Item</title>          <==
4
5  <!--[if gte mso 9]><xml>
6  <mso:CustomDocumentProperties>
7  <mso:TemplateHidden msdt:dt="string">0</mso:TemplateHidden>
```

Add the external content type managed properties to the Man-agedProperties tag:

'ProductSubCategory':'ProductSubCategory','ProductN
umber':'ProductNumber',

(see code examples on www.SteveTheManMann.com)

In the javascript code block, rename the hover panel:

```
if('isNull(ctx.CurrentItem) && 'isNull(ctx.ClientControl)){
    var id = ctx.ClientControl.get_nextUniqueId();
    var itemId = id + Srch.U.Ids.item;
    var hoverId = id + Srch.U.Ids.hover;
    var hoverUrl = "~sitecollection/_catalogs/masterpage/Display Templates/Search/Item_Product_HoverPanel.js";
    $setResultItem(itemId, ctx.CurrentItem);
    if(ctx.CurrentItem.IsContainer){
        ctx.CurrentItem.csr_Icon = Srch.U.getFolderIconUrl();
    }
    ctx.currentItem_ShowHoverPanelCallback = Srch.U.getShowHoverPanelCallback(itemId, hoverId, hoverUrl);
    ctx.currentItem_HideHoverPanelCallback = Srch.U.getHideHoverPanelCallback();
```

You will create the hover panel file in the next section.

Rename the data-displaytemplate:

```
<div id="_#= $htmlEncode(itemId) =#_" name="Item" data-displaytemplate="ProductItem" class=
_#=ctx.RenderBody(ctx)=#_
    <div id="_#= $htmlEncode(hoverId) =#_" class="ms-srch-hover-outerContainer"></div>
</div>
```

In the javascript code block, I create variables that determine if there is data in the managed property fields:

```
<!--#
    if(!$isNull(ctx.CurrentItem) && !$isNull(ctx.ClientControl)){
        var id = ctx.ClientControl.get_nextUniqueId();
        var itemId = id + Srch.U.Ids.item;
        var hoverId = id + Srch.U.Ids.hover;
        var hoverUrl = "~sitecollection/_catalogs/masterpage/Display Templates/Search/Item_Product_HoverPanel.js";
        $setResultItem(itemId, ctx.CurrentItem);
        if(ctx.CurrentItem.IsContainer){
            ctx.CurrentItem.csr_Icon = Srch.U.getFolderIconUrl();

        }

        var has_name = !$isEmptyString(ctx.CurrentItem.ProductName);
        var has_model = !$isEmptyString(ctx.CurrentItem.ProductModel);
        var has_number = !$isEmptyString(ctx.CurrentItem.ProductNumber);
        var has_category = !$isEmptyString(ctx.CurrentItem.ProductCategory);

        ctx.currentItem_ShowHoverPanelCallback = Srch.U.getShowHoverPanelCallback(itemId, hoverId, hoverUrl);
        ctx.currentItem_HideHoverPanelCallback = Srch.U.getHideHoverPanelCallback();
#-->
```

var has_name = !$isEmptyString(ctx.CurrentItem.ProductName);

var has_model = !$isEmptyString(ctx.CurrentItem.ProductModel);

var has_number = !$isEmptyString(ctx.CurrentItem.ProductNumber);

var has_category = !$isEmptyString(ctx.CurrentItem.ProductCategory);

Remove the ctx.RenderBody line:

```
        <div id="_#= $htmlEncode(itemId) =#_" name="It
            _#=ctx.RenderBody(ctx)=#_
            <div id="_#= $htmlEncode(hoverId) =#_" cl
        </div>
<!--#_
    }
#-->
```

For each managed property, create a code block similar to the following:

```
if(has_number == true) {

    <div id="ProductNumberField">
        <div id="ProductNumberValue" class="ms-srch-ellipsis" title="_#= ctx.CurrentItem.ProductNumber =#_">Product Number: _#= ctx.CurrentItem.ProductNumber =#_ </div>
    </div>

}
```

<!--#

   if(has_number == true) {

 #-->

        <div id="ProductNumberField">

          <div id="ProductNumberValue" class="ms-srch-ellipsis" title="_#= ctx.CurrentItem.ProductNumber =#_">Product Number: _#= ctx.CurrentItem.ProductNumber =#_ </div>

     </div>

<!--#

   }

 #-->

Code examples are available on www.SteveTheManMann.com.

```
<div id="_#= $htmlEncode(itemId) =#_" name="Item" data-displaytemplate="ProductItem" class="ms-srch-item" onmouseover="_#= ctx.currentItem_ShowHoverPanelCallback =#_" onmouseout="_#=

    if(has_number == true) {

        <div id="ProductNumberField">
            <div id="ProductNumberValue" class="ms-srch-ellipsis" title="_#= ctx.CurrentItem.ProductNumber =#_">Product Number: _#= ctx.CurrentItem.ProductNumber =#_ </div>
        </div>

    }

    if(has_name == true) {

        <div id="ProductNameField">
            <div id="ProductNameValue" class="ms-srch-ellipsis" title="_#= ctx.CurrentItem.ProductName =#_">Product Name: _#= ctx.CurrentItem.ProductName =#_ </div>
        </div>

    }

    if(has_model == true) {

        <div id="ProductModelField">
            <div id="ProductModelValue" class="ms-srch-ellipsis" title="_#= ctx.CurrentItem.ProductModel =#_">Product Model: _#= ctx.CurrentItem.ProductModel =#_ </div>
        </div>

    }
```

Save the html file.

Step 13: Create an Item Hover Panel

Back in the listing of display templates, locate and select the Item_Default_HoverPanel files. Right-click and select Copy:

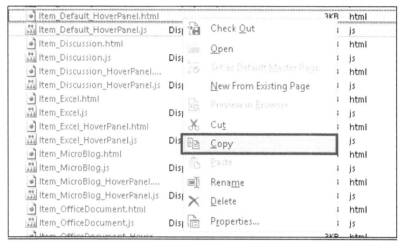

Right-click again and select Paste:

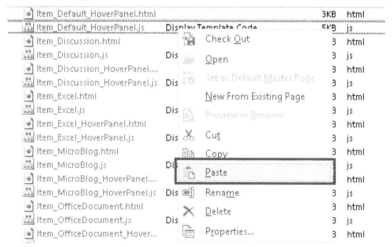

Rename the html file:

SharePoint automatically renames the .js file:

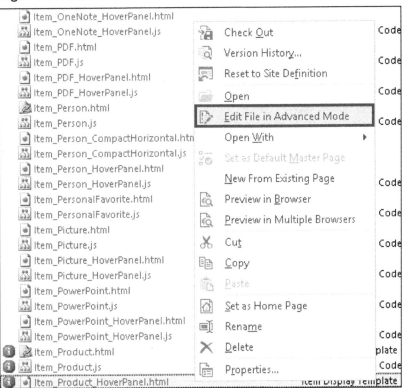

Item_Product.html	Item Display Template
Item_Product.js	Display Template Code
Item_Product_HoverPanel.html	Item Display Template
Item_Product_HoverPanel.js	Display Template Code

Right click the html file and select Edit File in Advanced Mode:

Item_OneNote_HoverPanel.html		
Item_OneNote_HoverPanel.js	Check Out	Code
Item_PDF.html	Version History...	
Item_PDF.js	Reset to Site Definition	Code
Item_PDF_HoverPanel.html		
Item_PDF_HoverPanel.js	Open	Code
Item_Person.html	Edit File in Advanced Mode	
Item_Person.js		Code
Item_Person_CompactHorizontal.htn	Open With ▶	
Item_Person_CompactHorizontal.js	Set as Default Master Page	
Item_Person_HoverPanel.html	New From Existing Page	
Item_Person_HoverPanel.js		Code
Item_PersonalFavorite.html	Preview in Browser	
Item_PersonalFavorite.js	Preview in Multiple Browsers	Code
Item_Picture.html		
Item_Picture.js	Cut	Code
Item_Picture_HoverPanel.html	Copy	
Item_Picture_HoverPanel.js	Paste	Code
Item_PowerPoint.html		
Item_PowerPoint.js	Set as Home Page	Code
Item_PowerPoint_HoverPanel.html	Rename	
Item_PowerPoint_HoverPanel.js		Code
Item_Product.html	Delete	plate
Item_Product.js	Properties...	Code
Item_Product_HoverPanel.html		Item Display Template

Rename the title:

```
1  <html xmlns:mso="urn:schemas-microsoft-com:office:office"
2  <head>
3  <title>Product Hover Panel</title>
4
5  <!--[if gte mso 9]><xml>
6  <mso:CustomDocumentProperties>
```

Copy and paste the ManagedPropertyMapping from the item display template created in the previous section:

```xml
<!--[if gte mso 9]><xml>
<mso:CustomDocumentProperties>
<mso:TemplateHidden msdt:dt="string">0</mso:TemplateHidden>
<mso:MasterPageDescription msdt:dt="string">Displays the default hover panel template.</mso:MasterPageDescription>
<mso:ContentTypeId msdt:dt="string">0x0101002039C03B61C64EC4A04F5361F385106603</mso:ContentTypeId>
<mso:TargetControlType msdt:dt="string">;#SearchHoverPanel;#</mso:TargetControlType>
<mso:HtmlDesignAssociated msdt:dt="string">1</mso:HtmlDesignAssociated>
<mso:ManagedPropertyMapping msdt:dt="string">'ProductSubCategory':'ProductSubCategory','ProductNumber':
'Title':'Title','Path':'Path','Description':'Description','EditorOWSUSER':
<mso:HtmlDesignConversionSucceeded msdt:dt="string">True</mso:HtmlDesignConversionSucceeded>
<mso:HtmlDesignStatusAndPreview msdt:dt="string">http://sp2013srv/sites/SearchCenter/_catalogs/masterpage/Display%20Templates/Search
```

Rename the Default entries:

```
<body>
    <div id="Item Product HoverPanel">
<!--#

    var i = 0;
    var id = ctx.CurrentItem.csr_id;
    ctx.CurrentItem.csr_ShowViewLibrary = !Srch.U.isWebPage(ctx.CurrentItem.FileExtension);
    if(ctx.CurrentItem.IsContainer)
    {

        ctx.CurrentItem.csr_FileType = Srch.Res.ct_Folder
    }

    ctx.currentItem_ShowChangedBySnippet = true;

_#-->
        <div class="ms-srch-hover-innerContainer ms-srch-hover-standardSize" id="_#= $htmlEncode(id + HP.ids.inner) =#_ ">
            <div class="ms-srch-hover-arrowBorder" id="_#= $htmlEncode(id + HP.ids.arrowBorder) =#_ "></div>
            <div class="ms-srch-hover-arrow" id="_#= $htmlEncode(id + HP.ids.arrow) =#_ "></div>
            <div class="ms-srch-hover-content" id="_#= $htmlEncode(id + HP.ids.content) =#_ " data-displaytemplate="ProductHoverPanel">
                <div id="_#= $htmlEncode(id + HP.ids.header) =#_ " class="ms-srch-hover-header">
                    _#= ctx.RenderHeader(ctx) =#_
```

Create variables for the managed properties you wish to display in the hover panel:

```
var has_name = !$isEmptyString(ctx.CurrentItem.ProductName);
var has_description = !$isEmptyString(ctx.CurrentItem.ProductDescription);
var has_color = !$isEmptyString(ctx.CurrentItem.ProductColor);
var has_listprice = !$isEmptyString(ctx.CurrentItem.ProductListPrice);
var has_category = !$isEmptyString(ctx.CurrentItem.ProductCategory);
var has_subcategory = !$isEmptyString(ctx.CurrentItem.ProductSubCategory);
```

Remove the Render Header <div>:

```
        <div class="ms-srch-hover-content" id="_#= $htmlEncode(id + HP.ids.content) =#_ " data-displaytemplate="ProductHoverPanel">
            <div id="_#= $htmlEncode(id + HP.ids.header) =#_ " class="ms-srch-hover-header">
                _#= ctx.RenderHeader(ctx) =#_
            </div>
            <div id="_#= $htmlEncode(id + HP.ids.body) =#_ " class="ms-srch-hover-body">
<!--#
```

Remove the ctx.RenderBody line:

```
<div class="ms-srch-hover-innerContainer ms-srch-hover-star
    <div class="ms-srch-hover-arrowBorder" id="_#= $htmlEnc
    <div class="ms-srch-hover-arrow" id="_#= $htmlEncode(i
    <div class="ms-srch-hover-content" id="_#= $htmlEncode
        <div id="_#= $htmlEncode(id + HP.ids.header) =#_"
            _#= ctx.RenderHeader(ctx) =#_
        </div>
        <div id="_#= $htmlEncode(id + HP.ids.body) =#_" cl
            _#= ctx.RenderBody(ctx) =#_
        </div>
        <div id="_#= $htmlEncode(id + HP.ids.actions) =#_"
            _#= ctx.RenderFooter(ctx) =#_
        </div>
    </div>
</div>
```

Again, add code blocks for each managed property. Example files are located on www.SteveTheManMann.com:

```
<div id="_#= $htmlEncode(id + HP.ids.body) =#_" class="ms-srch-hover-body">

    if(has_name == true) {

        <div id="ProductNameField">
            <div id="ProductNameValue" class="ms-srch-ellipsis" style="font-weight:bold"
        </div>

    }

    if(has_description == true) {

        <div id="ProductDescriptionField">
            <div id="ProductDescriptionValue" class="ms-srch-ellipsis" title="_#= ctx.Cur
        </div>

    }

    if(has_color == true) {

        <div id="ProductColorField">
            <div id="ProductColorValue" class="ms-srch-ellipsis" title="_#= ctx.Currentl
        </div>

    }
```

Save the file.

Step 14: Update the Result Type to Use the New Display Template

Navigate to your Search Center and select Site Settings from the Settings menu.

Under the Site Collection Administration section, click on the Search Result Types link:

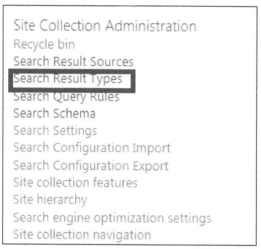

Locate the external content type Result Type and select Edit from the drop-down menu:

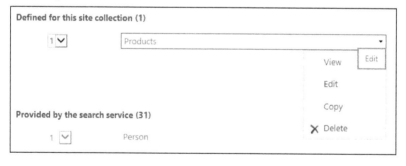

Change the What should these results look like? to the new display template created in the previous sections:

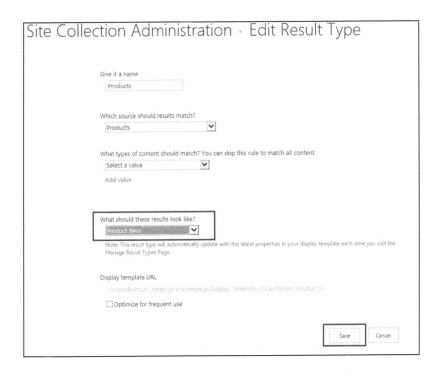

Click Save.

Step 15: Test the Item Display Template and Hover Panel

Navigate to your Search Center and perform a search within the new results page:

The results are shown with the managed property values and the hover panel displays additional information.

Conclusion

This guide demonstrated an end-to-end solution involving the integration of external data from SQL Server into SharePoint 2013 leveraging Business Data Connectivity Services. I hope you found this guide helpful and easy to follow. If there are any questions, issues, or concerns, please send them to steve@stevethemanmann.com.

Volume 3

How To Enhance Video Search Results in SharePoint 2013

STEVEN MANN

How To Enhance Video Search Results in SharePoint 2013

Copyright © 2013 by Steven Mann

Trademarks

Screenshots of Microsoft Products and Services

Warning and Disclaimer

Introduction

This guide explains some easy and simple options that you may wish to incorporate into your search center to enhance the querying and display of video based search results in SharePoint 2013.

Reference links and source code are available on www.stevethemanmann.com:

Implementing a Videos Query Rule

In SharePoint 2013 Search there are several out-of-the-box query rules to display ranked result blocks of various result types (.e.g Word, Excel, PowerPoint, etc.). These are triggered based on specific action terms that appear either in the beginning or end of a search query (or both). However, Videos is not one of them.

Therefore, it would be nice if someone performed a search query using "video" or "videos" that a promoted result block of video results would appear at the top of the results. Easier done than said!

Navigate to your Site Settings from within your Search Center site collection and click on Search Query Rules under Site Collection Administration:

Site Collection Administration
Recycle bin
Search Result Sources
Search Result Types
Search Query Rules
Search Schema
Search Settings
Search Configuration Import
Search Configuration Export
Site collection features
Site hierarchy

Select Local SharePoint Results (System) as the Result Source:

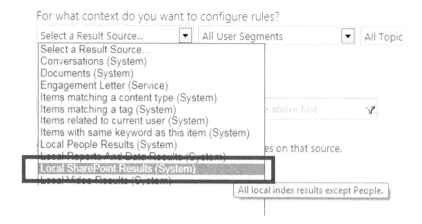

Click on the New Query Rule link:

Add the Rule Name, select Query Contains Action Term, enter "video;videos" in the Action term is one of these phrases:

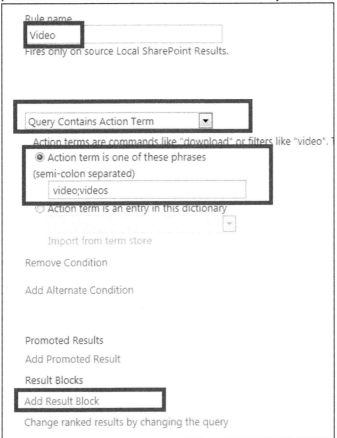

Click on Add Result Block.

Modify the Block Title. Change Search this Source to Local Video Results (System) and increase the amount of Items as desired (I used 6). Expand the Settings section.

Select the "More" link since there is already a Video Results page and enter the value shown in the image below. Select Video Item as the Display Template:

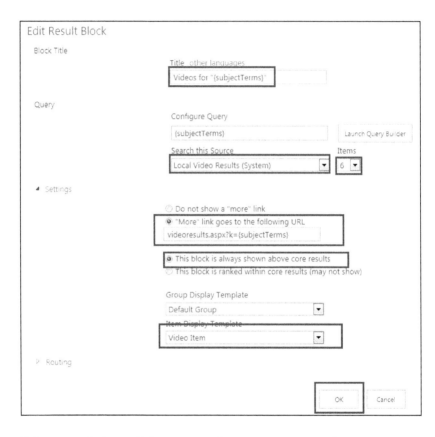

Click OK and then click Save on the New Query Rule page.

Navigate to your Search Center main page and perform a search using "videos" in the query:

Videos for "sharepoint"

SharePoint Youtube

  /Video Library/SharePoint Youtube

SharePoint in Plain English

Mann, Steven Enterprise App Engineer, Application
Development ...

  /Videos/SharePoint in Plain English

SharePoint Video

  /sites/Videos/Videos/SharePoint Video

What is **SharePoint**

Mann, Steven Enterprise App Engineer, Application
Development ...

  /sites/Videos/Videos/What is SharePoint

Top Benefits of **SharePoint** 2013

Mann, Steven Enterprise App Engineer, Application
Development ...

  /sites/.../Videos/Top Benefits of SharePoint 2013

Tour **SharePoint** 2013 User Interfaces

Mann, Steven Enterprise App Engineer, Application
Development ...

  /sites/.../Tour SharePoint 2013 User Interfaces

The video result block appears at the top and displays the video results. The results show hover panels when moused over.

Display Video Results Horizontally

There is another way to display these results using an out-of-the-box horizontal video display template. If you go back into your Search Query Rules, edit the Video query, and then edit the Result Block, you may change the Display Template setting to just the Video entry:

Now the results are displayed horizontally along the top:

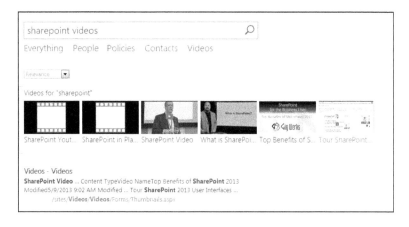

This presents well but there is no hover! You can easily modify the template (or make a new copy as the recommended approach) to display the hover. Those steps are in the next section.

Adding a Hover Panel to the Video Horizontal Display Template

The previous section demonstrated how to display Video results in a horizontal fashion using the out-of-the-box Video horizontal template. However, this display does not incorporate a hover panel and thus nothing pops up when mousing over the results. No problem. You may add a hover panel to the template in just a few easy steps.

First, navigate to the Search Center display templates via SharePoint Designer 2013, similar to the process explained in Appendix A. For simplicity, these steps discuss modifying the display template file in-place but the recommended approach would be to make a copy and use that.

Locate the Item_Video_CompactHorizontal.html file, right-click, and select Edit File in Advanced Mode:

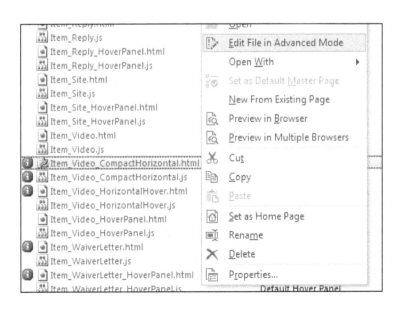

Paste this code at the top as shown in the image below:

```
var id = ctx.ClientControl.get_nextUniqueId();
var itemId = id + Srch.U.Ids.item;
var hoverId = id + Srch.U.Ids.hover;
var hoverUrl = "~sitecollection/_catalogs/masterpage/Display Tem-
plates/Search/Item_Video_HoverPanel.js";
$setResultItem(itemId, ctx.CurrentItem);
ctx.currentItem_ShowHoverPanelCallback =
Srch.U.getShowHoverPanelCallback(itemId, hoverId, hoverUrl);
ctx.currentItem_HideHoverPanelCallback = Srch.U.getHideHoverPanelCallback();
```

Notice this is using the out-of-the-box Item_Video_HoverPanel .

Next, scroll down to the main <div> and change the id to use _#= $htmlEncode(itemId) =#_

```
mediaDuration.overrideValueRenderer(formatTimeFromSeconds):
 _#-->
    <div class="ms-srch-video-intent ms-srch-video-intent-container" id="_#= $htmlEncode(itemId) =#_" data-displaytemplate="VideoIntentIt
        <div id="_#= $htmlEncode(hoverId) =#_" class="ms-srch-hover-outerContainer"></div>
        <div class="ms-srch-video-results-centered ms-srch-video-intent">
            <a clicktype="Result" href="_#= linkUrl =#_" title="_#= $htmlEncode(line1.value) =#_" id="_#= pathId =#_">
                _#= imageMarkup =#_
            </a>
        </div>
        <div class="ms-srch-video-intent-data">
            <h3>
                <a clicktype="Result" href="_#= linkUrl =#_" title="_#= $htmlEncode(line1.value) =#_" class="ms-srch-video-intent ms-srch
                    _#= line1 =#_
                </a>
            </h3>
<!--#_
if (!mediaDuration.isNull)
 _#-->
                    _#= mediaDuration =#_
```

Add the following code to that very same <div> tag:

onmouseover=" #= ctx.currentItem_ShowHoverPanelCallback =# "
onmouseout=" #= ctx.currentItem_HideHoverPanelCallback =# "

```
itm" onmouseover="_#= ctx.currentItem_ShowHoverPanelCallback =#_" onmouseout="_#= ctx.currentItem_HideHoverPanelCallback =#_">




h-video-results ms-srch-item-link ms-noWrap" id="_#= line1Id =#_">
```

Now add the following <div> after the first <div>:

<div id=" #= $htmlEncode(hoverId) =# " class="ms-srch-hover-outerContainer"></div>

```
 _#-->
<!--#_
 _#-->
    if (!Srch.U.n(ctx.CurrentItem.ParentTableReference) && ctx.CurrentItem.ParentTableReference.TotalRows > 1) {

    <div id="_#= $htmlEncode(itemId) =#_" name="Item" class="ms-srch-peopleaintentItem" onmouseover="_#= ctx.currentIt
        <div id="_#= $htmlEncode(hoverId) =#_" class="ms-srch-hover-outerContainer"></div>
        <div id="VideoCard">
            <ul id="VideoCard">
                <li class="ms-srch-video-itemthumbnail">
                    <a clicktype="Result" href="_#= titleLinkUrl =#_" id="_#= thumbnailPathId =#_">
                        _#= imageMarkup =#_
                        <div class="ms-srch-video-playbutton ms-srch-video-playbutton-result"><span></span></div>
                    </a>
                </li>
                <li class="ms-srch-video-itemmain">
                    <h3>
                        <div id="_#= $htmlEncode(id + Srch.U.Ids.title) =#_" class="ms-srch-item-title">
                            <h3>
                                <a clicktype="Result" id="_#= $htmlEncode(id + Srch.U.Ids.titleLink) =#_" href="_#= titleLinkU
                                    _#= Srch.U.trimTitle(title, maxTitleLengthInChars, termsToUse) =#_
                                </a>
                            </h3>
                        </div>
                    </li>
                </ul>
            </div>
        </li>
    </div>
<!--#_
```

Save the changes to the template.

Navigate to your Search Center and perform a search that re-turns Video results:

Hovering over the results shows the hover panel preview!!!

Conclusion

It is very easy to customize and enhance search results within SharePoint 2013. This guide focused on video based search results. I hope you found this information useful and easy to use. If there are any questions or problems, please send them to steve@stevethemanmann.com

Volume 4

How To Implement Remote Blob Storage in SharePoint 2013

STEVEN MANN

How To Implement Remote Blob Storage in SharePoint 2013

Trademarks

Screenshots of Microsoft Products and Services

Warning and Disclaimer

Introduction

This guide outlines steps and configurations to implement Remote Blob Storage (RBS) in SharePoint 2013 using SQL Server 2012.

One of the advantages with the latest SharePoint versions and SQL Server versions is the ability to implement RBS using the FileStream Provider. This allows for documents and files that are larger than a specified amount of bytes (default 100KB) to be stored on a connected file system of the SQL Server box instead of inside the database itself. The overall advantage is keeping your content databases smaller and more manageable.

Reference links and source code are available on www.stevethemanmann.com:

Step 1: Enable File Stream on the SQL Server

On the SQL Server 2012 box, open SQL Server Configurations Manager.

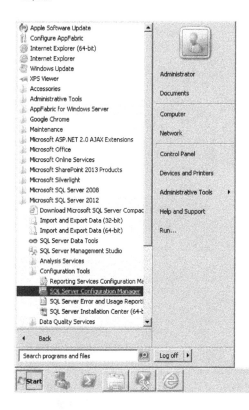

Select SQL Server Services from the left pane. Right-click on the SQL Server process in the right window and select Properties:

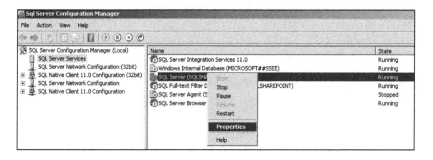

The SQL Server Properties dialog appears. Select the FILESTREAM tab and check all of the check boxes:

Click OK.

Start SQL Management Studio and open a new query window.

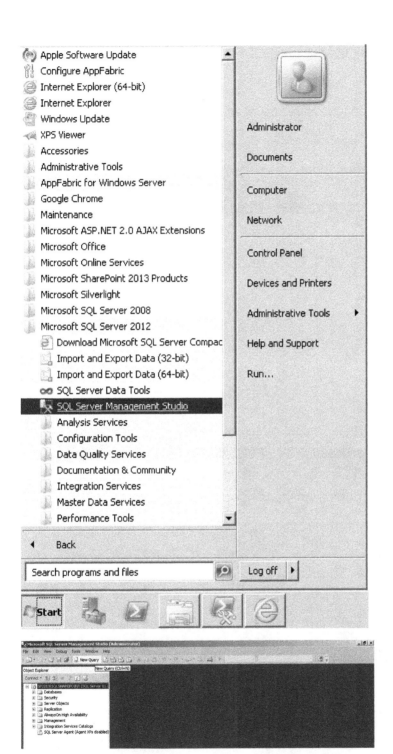

Execute the following two SQL Statements (on any database):

EXEC sp_configure filestream_access_level, 2

RECONFIGURE

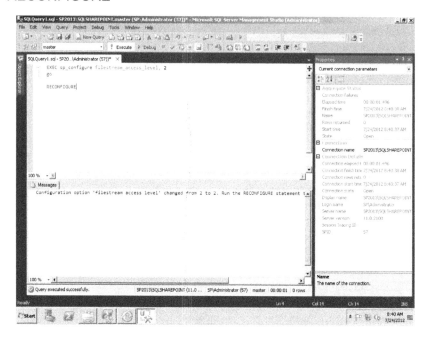

Using your content database open a new query:

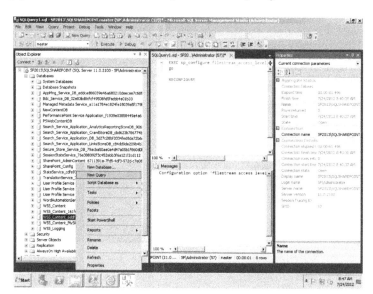

Create the master key using the following SQL:

if not exists (select * from sys.symmetric_keys where name
= N'##MS_DatabaseMasterKey##')
    create master key encryption by password = N'Admin Key
Password !2#4'

```
SQLQuery2.sql - SP20...\Administrator (65))*  ×
 use WSS_Content_6ddf1a64a957436589e0a80ad67f9301

 if not exists (select * from sys.symmetric_keys where name =
     N'##MS_DatabaseMasterKey##')create master key encryption by
     password = N'Admin Key Password !2#4'
```

**It is very important that the password is !2#4 - RBS will not
work properly if this is not the password used.**

Create a new filegroup for the RBS:

if not exists (select groupname from sysfilegroups where group-
name=N'RBSFilestreamProvider')
    alter database [<your content database>]
    add filegroup RBSFilestreamProvider contains filestream

```
SQLQuery3.sql - SP20...Administrator (131))*   SQLQuery2.sql - SP20...\Administrator (52))*  ×  SQLQuery1.sql - SP20...\Administrator (57))*
 if not exists (select groupname from sysfilegroups where groupname=N'RBSFilestreamProvider')
 alter database WSS_Content_6ddf1a64a957436589e0a80ad67f9301 add
     filegroup RBSFilestreamProvider contains filestream




100 %  ▾ ◀
```

Add the "file" using the following SQL:

alter database [<your content database>]
add file (name = RBSFilestreamFile, filename=
'c:\SPBlobStorage')
    to filegroup RBSFilestreamProvider

The "file" is a folder on a connected drive. It can be a local drive on the SQL Server or an attached iSCSI drive. The folder cannot exist already. Executing the SQL statement above automatically creates the folder specified on the drive specified.

Step 2: Install RBS on the DB and Web/Application Servers

The RBS bits need to be installed on the database server and on each Web server and Application server that exist in the Share-Point farm. The RBS bits are a separate installation as part of the SQL Server 2012 Feature Pack. You can access the feature pack for SQL Server 2012 here. (http://www.microsoft.com/en-us/download/details.aspx?id=29065)

Scroll down on the feature pack download page and locate the RBS download:

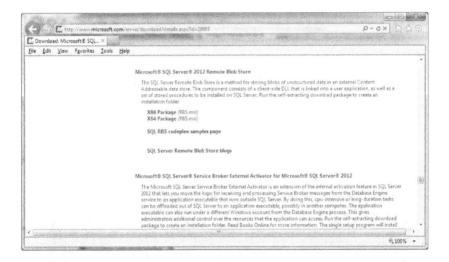

Download the appropriate package (hopefully x64) and save it in a central location.

For the first web server (or database server), create a new batch file, in the same location as you downloaded RBS.msi, using the following code (all on one line - no line breaks):

msiexec /qn /lvx* rbs_install_log.txt /i RBS.msi

TRUSTSERVERCERTIFICATE=true FILEGROUP=PRIMARY
DBNAME="<ContentDbName>"
DBINSTANCE="<DBInstanceName>"
FILESTREAMFILEGROUP=RBSFilestreamProvider
FILESTREAMSTORENAME=FileStreamStore

Open a Command Prompt and execute the first batch file:

Verify success by reviewing the rbs_install_log.txt file that was generated in the same folder. The completion message is not the very last thing but it is towards the end of the log:

```
rbs_install_log.txt - Notepad
File Edit Format View Help
- {B7861226-98CF-4CB8-A999-1D05DC2DE3E2}
ered = 1
  Note: 1: 1707
  Product: Microsoft SQL Server 2012 Remote BLOB Store -- Installation completed successfully.

  Windows Installer installed the product. Product Name: Microsoft SQL Server 2012 Remote BLOB Store . Pr

  Deferring clean up of packages/files, if any exist
  MainEngineThread is returning 0
  RESTART MANAGER: Session closed.
  No System Restore sequence number for this installation.
  9:19:32 ===
  User policy value 'DisableRollback' is 0
  Machine policy value 'DisableRollback' is 0
  Incrementing counter to disable shutdown. Counter after increment: 0
  Note: 1: 1402 2: HKEY_LOCAL_MACHINE\Software\Microsoft\Windows\CurrentVersion\Installer\Rollback\Script
  Note: 1: 1402 2: HKEY_LOCAL_MACHINE\Software\Microsoft\Windows\CurrentVersion\Installer\Rollback\Script
  Decrementing counter to disable shutdown. If counter >= 0, shutdown will be denied. Counter after decr
  Restoring environment variables
  Destroying RemoteAPI object.
```

On all of the other web servers and application servers, place the following code into a batch file (again no line breaks):

msiexec /qn /lvx* rbs_install_log.txt /i RBS.msi
DBNAME="ContentDbName" DBINSTANCE="DBInstanceName"
ADDLOCAL="Client,Docs,Maintainer,ServerScript,FilestreamClien
t,FilestreamServer"

```
Install_RBS_WEB.bat - Notepad
File Edit Format View Help
msiexec /qn /lvx* rbs_install_log.txt /i RBS.msi DBNAME="WSS_Content_6ddf1a64a957436589e0a80ad67f9301"
DBINSTANCE="SP2013\SQLSHAREPOINT"
ADDLOCAL="Client,Docs,Maintainer,ServerScript,FilestreamClient,FilestreamServer"
```

Open a Command Prompt and execute the second batch file on each web server and application server:

```
Administrator: C:\Windows\system32\cmd.exe - Install_RBS_Web
Y:\spblob>dir
 Volume in drive Y is Data
 Volume Serial Number is DEC1-B9DE

 Directory of Y:\spblob

07/24/2012  09:23 AM    <DIR>          .
07/24/2012  09:23 AM    <DIR>          ..
07/24/2012  09:18 AM                260 Install_RBS_SQL.bat
07/24/2012  09:23 AM                217 Install_RBS_WEB.bat
07/24/2012  09:06 AM          5,242,880 RBS.msi
07/24/2012  09:19 AM          1,424,736 rbs_install_log.txt
               4 File(s)      6,668,093 bytes
               2 Dir(s)  37,603,364,864 bytes free

Y:\spblob>Install_RBS_Web

Y:\spblob>msiexec /qn /lvx* rbs_install_log.txt /i RBS.msi DBNAME="WSS_Content_6
ddf1a64a957436589e0a80ad67f9301" DBINSTANCE="SP2013\SQLSHAREPOINT" ADDLOCAL="Cli
ent,Docs,Maintainer,ServerScript,FilestreamClient,FilestreamServer"
_
```

Step 3: Enable RBS on the Content Database

To enable RBS on the content database, you must use PowerShell. Therefore, open up PowerShell or Notepad and create the following PowerShell Script:

```
$cdb = Get-SPContentDatabase -
WebApplication "<Web Application Name>"
$rbss = $cdb.RemoteBlobStorageSettings
$rbss.Installed()
$rbss.Enable()
$rbss.SetActiveProviderName($rbss.GetProviderNames()[0])
$rbss
```

You may also add $rbss.MinimumBlobStorageSize=1048576 to increase the minimum file size that will be considered for RBS. The example number shows 1MB.

Save the script as a .ps1 file and then open the SharePoint 2013
Management Shell:

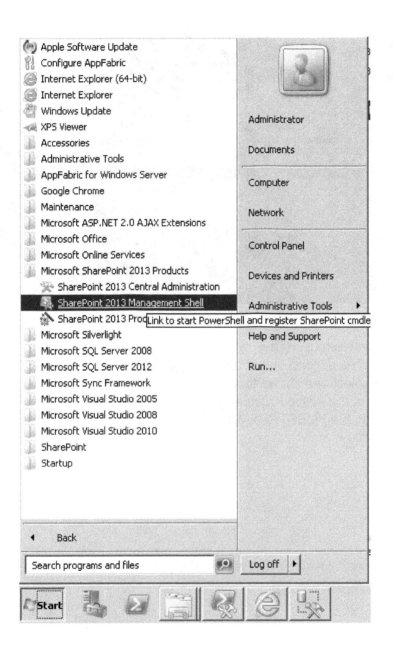

Execute the script:

```
Administrator: SharePoint 2013 Management Shell                    _ □ ×
PS Y:\spblob> dir


    Directory: Y:\spblob


Mode                LastWriteTime       Length Name
----                -------------       ------ ----
-a---        7/24/2012    9:48 AM          204 Enable_RBS.ps1
-a---        7/24/2012    9:18 AM          260 Install_RBS_SQL.bat
-a---        7/24/2012    9:23 AM          217 Install_RBS_WEB.bat
-a---        7/24/2012    9:06 AM      5242880 RBS.msi
-a---        7/24/2012    9:24 AM       578926 rbs_install_log.txt


PS Y:\spblob> .\Enable_RBS.ps1
True

              Enabled ActiveProviderName  MinimumBlobStorageS UpgradedPersistedPr
                                                          ize operties
              ------- ------------------  ------------------- -------------------
                 True FilestreamStore                       0 {}


PS Y:\spblob> _
```

The first output is"True" which means RBS has been installed correctly. The second output displays the RemoteBlobStorageSet-
tings object and shows that RBS is enabled and displays the
name of the Active Provider (which should be the same name you
used as the FILESTREAMSTORENAME in the RBS installation
batch file.

Step 4: Test RBS

Now it's time to see this working in action! Navigate to your SharePoint site related to the content database you just configured. Open a document library:

Upload a bunch of documents into the document library:

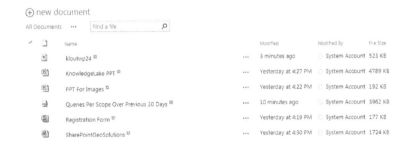

Investigate the folders within the local file system blob storage location:

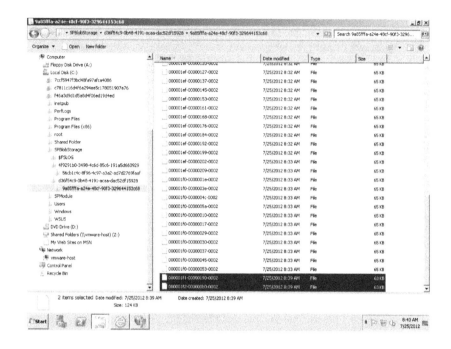

Files appear in small chunks. They will not be human readable.

Conclusion

This guide stepped you through the configurations to implement remote blob storage in SharePoint 2013 using SQL Server 2012. Enabling RBS with SharePoint 2013 is mostly configured on the SQL Server side and is possible because of the file stream provider. I hope you found the steps easy to follow and that this guide helped you implement RBS.

Volume 5

Finding Empty User Profile Properties in SharePoint 2013

STEVEN MANN

Finding Empty Profile Properties in SharePoint 2013

Trademarks

Screenshots of Microsoft Products and Services

Warning and Disclaimer

Introduction

This guide steps through SharePoint PowerShell scripting that may be used to loop through your User Profile properties in SharePoint 2013 and identify missing information. User Profiles contain information about your users in SharePoint. There are many properties that may or may not be populated. With missing information, it may be hard to find someone or get the proper People search results.

While you may use the same code to find any user profile property, the example outlined in this guide finds all people that do not have their PictureURL populated, that is, the user does not have an associated picture in SharePoint.

Reference links and source code are available on www.stevethemanmann.com:

Step 1: Define Dynamic Variables

Dynamic Settings
$mySiteUrl = "http://mysite.company.net"
$findProperty = "PictureUrl"

Step 2: Establish the Server Context

Obtain Context based on site

$mySiteHostSite = Get-SPSite $mySiteUrl

$mySiteHostWeb = $mySiteHostSite.OpenWeb()

$context = Get-SPServiceContext $mySiteHostSite

Step 3: Instantiate a ProfileManager Object and Retrieve all of the SharePoint User Profiles

Obtain Profiles from the Profile Manager
$profileManager = New-Object

     Mi-
crosoft.Office.Server.UserProfiles.UserProfileManager($context)

$AllProfiles = $profileManager.GetEnumerator()

$outputCollection = @()

Step 4: Loop through the profiles and retrieve

the account name (for identification purposes) and the property you are interested in finding

```
# Loop through profiles and retrieve the desired property

foreach ($profile in $AllProfiles)

{

    $output = New-Object System.Object

    $output | Add-Member -type NoteProperty -Name Account-
Name -Value $profile["AccountName"].ToString()

    $output | Add-Member -type NoteProperty -Name $findProper-
ty -Value $profile[$findProperty]

    $outputCollection += $output

}
```

Step 5: List out the collection items that do not have a value for the property (ie. null):

```
# List all Accounts that do not contain the property

$outputCollection | Where-Object {[bool]$_.($findProperty) -ne
$true}
```

FULL SCRIPT

```powershell
# Dynamic Settings

$mySiteUrl = "http://mysite.company.net"

$findProperty = "PictureUrl"


Write-Host "Beginning Processing--`n"


# Obtain Context based on site

$mySiteHostSite = Get-SPSite $mySiteUrl

$mySiteHostWeb = $mySiteHostSite.OpenWeb()

$context = Get-SPServiceContext $mySiteHostSite


# Obtain Profiles from the Profile Manager

$profileManager = New-Object Mi-
crosoft.Office.Server.UserProfiles.UserProfileManager($context)

$AllProfiles = $profileManager.GetEnumerator()

$outputCollection = @()
```

```
# Loop through profiles and retrieve the desired property

foreach ($profile in $AllProfiles)

{

    $output = New-Object System.Object

    $output | Add-Member -type NoteProperty -Name Account-Name -
    Value $profile["AccountName"].ToString()

    $output | Add-Member -type NoteProperty -Name $findProp-erty -
    Value $profile[$findProperty]

    $outputCollection += $output

}


# List all Accounts that do not contain the property

$outputCollection | Where-Object {[bool]$_.($findProperty) -ne $true}
```

Conclusion

It is easy to use PowerShell to loop through User Profile Properties. The example in this guide identified all users who do not have a picture uploaded in their profile. You may use the full script to identify other user profile properties that may be missing information.

Volume 6

Installing and Configuring Office Web Apps Server in SharePoint 2013

STEVEN MANN

Installing and Configuring Office Web Apps Server in SharePoint 2013

Copyright © 2013 by Steven Mann

Trademarks

Screenshots of Microsoft Products and Services

Warning and Disclaimer

Introduction

This guide walks you through the installation and configuration of Office Web Apps Server integrated with SharePoint 2013. Both Windows Server 2008 R2 and Windows Server 2012 installations are explored.

Reference links and source code are available on www.stevethemanmann.com:

Step 1A: Prepare for Office Web Apps Server on Windows Server 2008 R2

If you are using Windows Server 2008 R2, you need to make sure the following is installed first:

- Windows Server 2008 R2 Service Pack 1
- .NET Framework 4.5
- Windows PowerShell 3.0
- KB2592525

Add the required server features using PowerShell:

```
Import-Module ServerManager
```

```
Add-WindowsFeature Web-Server,Web-WebServer,Web-
Common-Http,Web-Static-Content,Web-App-Dev,Web-Asp-
Net,Web-Net-Ext,Web-ISAPI-Ext,Web-ISAPI-Filter,Web-
Includes,Web-Security,Web-Windows-Auth,Web-
Filtering,Web-Stat-Compression,Web-Dyn-
Compression,Web-Mgmt-Console,Ink-Handwriting,IH-Ink-
Support
```

If the output shows that a restart is needed (Restart Needed = Yes), restart your server before continuing.

Step 1B: Prepare for Office Web Apps Server on Windows Server 2012

Preparing your server on Windows Server 2012 is slightly different. You need to add the features as follows:

Import-Module ServerManager

Add-WindowsFeature Web-Server,Web-Mgmt-Tools,Web-Mgmt-Console,Web-WebServer,Web-Common-Http,Web-Default-Doc,Web-Static-Content,Web-Performance,Web-Stat-Compression,Web-Dyn-Compression,Web-Security,Web-Filtering,Web-Windows-Auth,Web-App-Dev,Web-Net-Ext45,Web-Asp-Net45,Web-ISAPI-Ext,Web-ISAPI-Filter,Web-Includes,InkandHandwritingServices

If the output shows that a restart is needed, restart your server before continuing.

Step 2: Download and Install Office Web Apps Server 2013 (October 2012 Release)

Download and install the Office Web Apps Server 2013 October 2013 Release (http://www.microsoft.com/en-us/download/details.aspx?id=35489)

Step 3: Download and Install Office Web Apps Server 2013 Public Update (March 2013 Update)

Next, download and install the Office Web Apps Server update located at: http://www.microsoft.com/en-us/download/details.aspx?id=36981

Step 4: Create the Office Web Apps Farm

Now you need to create the new Office Web Apps Farm on the server via PowerShell:

```
Import-Module OfficeWebApps

New-OfficeWebAppsFarm -InternalURL http://servername
-AllowHttp -EditingEnabled
```

Confirm the Editing operation:

The operation results with all of the properties displayed:

```
FarmOU                              :
InternalURL                         : http://stvspsm13/
ExternalURL                         :
AllowHTTP                           : True
SSLOffloaded                        : False
CertificateName                     :
EditingEnabled                      : True
LogLocation                         : C:\ProgramData\Microsoft\OfficeWebApps\Data\Logs\ULS
LogRetentionInDays                  : 7
LogVerbosity                        :
Proxy                               :
CacheLocation                       : C:\ProgramData\Microsoft\OfficeWebApps\Working\d
MaxMemoryCacheSizeInMB              : 75
DocumentInfoCacheSize               : 5000
CacheSizeInGB                       : 15
ClipartEnabled                      : False
TranslationEnabled                  : False
MaxTranslationCharacterCount        : 125000
TranslationServiceAppId             :
TranslationServiceAddress           :
RenderingLocalCacheLocation         : C:\ProgramData\Microsoft\OfficeWebApps\Working\waccache
RecycleActiveProcessCount           : 5
AllowCEIP                           : False
ExcelRequestDurationMax             : 300
ExcelSessionTimeout                 : 450
ExcelWorkbookSizeMax                : 10
ExcelPrivateBytesMax                : -1
ExcelConnectionLifetime             : 1800
ExcelExternalDataCacheLifetime      : 300
ExcelAllowExternalData              : True
ExcelWarnOnDataRefresh              : True
OpenFromUrlEnabled                  : False
OpenFromUncEnabled                  : True
OpenFromUrlThrottlingEnabled        : True
AllowHttpSecureStoreConnections     : False
Machines                            : {STVSPSM13}
```

The next step is to test the Office Web Apps server using a browser to confirm that http://servername/hosting/discovery produces a wopi-discovery response:

Now onto the SharePoint 2013 Farm!

Step 5: Bind SharePoint 2013 to Office Web Apps

Open the SharePoint 2013 Management Shell on one of your farm servers. Create the new binding using the following command:

New-SPWOPIBinding -ServerName <WacServerName> -AllowHTTP

Set the zone:

```
Set-SPWopiZone -zone "internal-http"
```

If you are using HTTP, you need to allow OAuth over HTTP by using the following commands:

$config = (Get-SPSecurityTokenServiceConfig)
$config.AllowOAuthOverHttp = $true
$config.Update()

Step 6: Verify SharePoint 2013 is Using Office Web Apps

Browse a document library with Office documents:

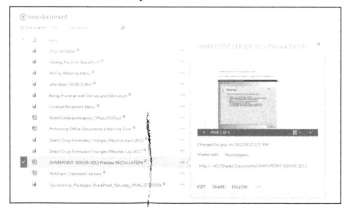

Search for Office documents: (may need to perform a full crawl before the preview kicks in)

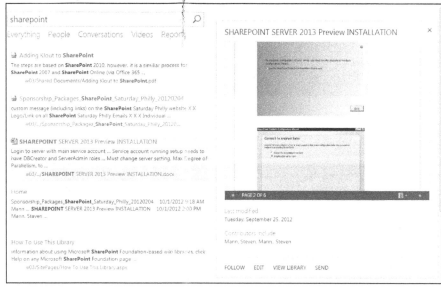

Conclusion

This guide walked through the steps to install and configure Office Web Apps Server for SharePoint 2013. It is surprising at times how easy it is to install and configure Office Web Apps Server in SharePoint 2013. I hope you found this guide useful and informative.

Volume 7

How to Enhance PDF Results and Previews in SharePoint 2013 Search

STEVEN MANN

How to Enhance PDF Results and Previews in SharePoint 2013 Search

Copyright © 2013 by Steven Mann

Trademarks

Screenshots of Microsoft Products and Services

Warning and Disclaimer

Introduction

This guide discusses the behaviors of PDF Document search results in SharePoint 2013 as well as various preview options. PDF
Document Previews in search results are possible both with and
without Office Web Apps Server 2013. This guide walks through
both options and demonstrates a hybrid approach as well.

Reference links and source code is available on
www.stevethemanmann.com:

PDF Handling Overview

SharePoint 2013 supports PDF documents out-of-the-box. Initially, web applications do not allow opening PDFs in the browser, however, by adding PDF as an allowed MIME type, browser rendering via Adobe is achieved.

Office Web Apps server provides Office document previews and rendering in Search results without the need for client applications installed (e.g. Word, Excel, etc.). However, once SharePoint is bound to Office Web Apps, PDF documents no longer open in the browser.

There are two workarounds –

1) Configure PDF items to render as Word Items which allows PDFs to open and preview in Search within Office Web Apps

2) Modify the PDF Item display template which allows PDFs to render in the browser via Adobe. Modify the PDF hover template to display previews.

These workarounds take care of Search, but PDFs will still open in the client application (e.g. Adobe) from Document Libraries. The solution here is an update to Office Web Apps. The February/March 2013 Update to Office Web Apps server supports opening PDFs from document libraries within Office Web Apps.

The following table summarizes the various PDF rendering and preview behaviors:

	Search PDF Preview	Search Open (clicking on result)	Document Library Open (clicking on Document)
Out of the Box (Strict Web App)	Available by modifying the Display Template	Opens in Adobe or associated client application	Opens in Adobe or associated client application
Out of the Box (Permissive Web App or Allowed Mime Type of PDF)	Available by modifying the Display Template	Opens in web browser and search term is passed into Adobe	Web Browser
Office Web Apps Server (October 2012 Release)	Two options: 1. Display template (shows in Adobe web) 2. Modify Result Type to use Word Item (shows in Word App Web)	Opens in Adobe or associated client application. Opens in Browser with modification of display template	Opens in Adobe or associated client application.
Office Web Apps Server (Feb/Mar 2013 Update)	Two options: 1. Display template (shows in Adobe web) 2. Modify Result Type to use Word Item (shows in Word App Web)	Opens in browser using Word Web App. Can use templates to display in Adobe Web.	Opens in browser using Word Web App. If not bound to WordPDF – Opens in Adobe or associated client application.

It is also worth mentioning that if Office Web Apps is not used for Search results of PDFs, the opening of PDFs in the browser passes the search terms into Adobe and thus finds the occurrences within the document. An example of this "search term pass-through" is displayed below:

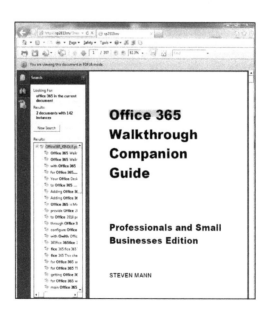

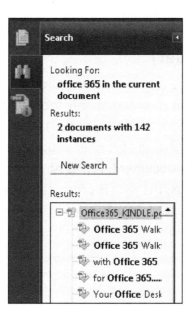

Based on my investigations and modifications, when using Office Web Apps server with SharePoint, there are two overall options when handling PDFs. One provides a more consistent user experience and the other provides the most functionality.

Most Consistent User Experience

The most consistent user experience would be to use Office Web Apps server (with the update) to enable opening of PDFs from libraries in the browser and to modify the search result type to render PDFs as Word Items which enables both preview and opening of the documents from Search results within Office Web Apps.

Most Functionality

The option that provides the most functionality is to use Office Web Apps for document libraries such that PDFs are opened within the browser but then use customized search templates to preview and open PDFs from Search results thus providing the search term pass-through functionality as described above. For the most consistent preview, use a customized copy of the Word item hover panel template.

The rest of this guide steps through the details and explains how to accomplish the various options and behaviors.

PDF Handling Out-Of-The-Box (without Office Web Apps Server)

Web Applications are created with the Browser File Handling option set to Strict. This means that only the default allowed MIME types (correlates to document types such Word, PDF, etc.) can open and display within the browser without prompting the user to Open or Save the document. PDF is not one of those default MIME types and thus, the user is prompted when attempting to open a PDF document:

The recommended way to enable PDFs to be opened in the browser is to add the MIME type to the allowed list of types by using PowerShell commands:

```
$webApplication = Get-SPWebApplication "http:/yourwebapplicationurl"
$webAppApplication.AllowedInlineDownloadedMimeTypes.Add("application/pdf")
$webApplication.Update()
```

Source:
http://social.technet.microsoft.com/wiki/contents/articles/8073.sharepoint-2010-and-2013-browser-file-handling-deep-dive.aspx#DownloadFunctions

The other easy option, which is not recommended, is to modify your web application (via Central Admin) and change the Browser File Handling property to Permissive:

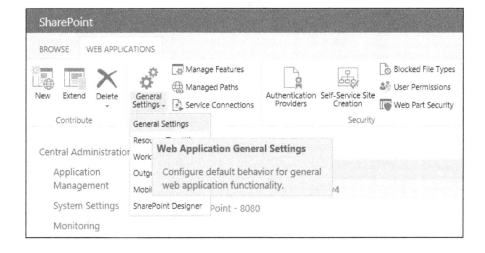

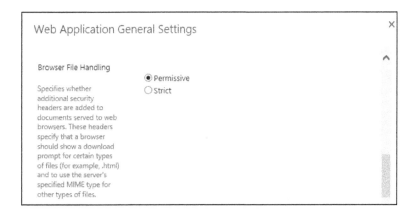

Either method will allow PDF files to be opened in the browser. A neat experience in search results is that the search term is passed into Adobe and the terms are highlighted in the document:

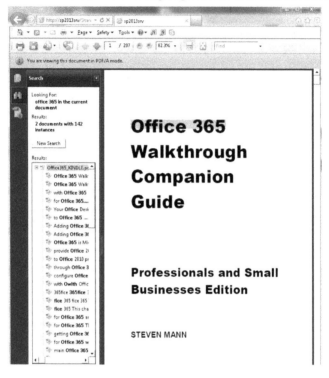

PDF Handling with Office Web Apps October 2012 Release Version

Once Office Web Apps is installed and configured, by surprise, PDF documents no longer open in the browser. Neither from document libraries nor from the search results. So there two options at this point (at least for the search results).

1. Copy the PDF Result Type and use the Word Item template for PDFs. This method both shows a preview and opens up PDF search results in the Office Web App's Word App Viewer. (See section in this guide for steps).

2. Use my original method for creating a PDF Preview to generate the preview by modifying the Display Templates. (See section in this guide for the steps).

Follow these steps to allow opening of the PDF document in the browser via Adobe (maintaining the search term pass-through functionality:

Modify the Item_PDF.html in the display templates folder. (see next sections for detailed steps on how to get to the templates)

Replace this line:

ctx.CurrentItem.csr_OpenControl = "PdfFile.OpenDocuments";

With this one:

ctx.CurrentItem.csr_OpenApp = "word";

```
if(!Srch.U.e(k)){
    ctx.CurrentItem.csr_Path = ctx.CurrentItem.Path + "&search=" + $urlKeyValueEncode(k);
}
ctx.CurrentItem.csr_Icon = Srch.U.getIconUrlByFileExtension(ctx.CurrentItem);
ctx.CurrentItem.csr_OpenControl = "PdfFile.OpenDocuments";
ctx.currentItem_ShowHoverPanelCallback = Srch.U.getShowHoverPanelCallback(itemId, hoverId, hoverUrl);
ctx.currentItem_HideHoverPanelCallback = Srch.U.getHideHoverPanelCallback();
```

```
if(!Srch.U.e(k)){
    ctx.CurrentItem.csr_Path = ctx.CurrentItem.Path + "#search=" + $urlKeyValueEncode(k);
}
ctx.CurrentItem.csr_Icon = Srch.U.getIconUrlByFileExtension(ctx.CurrentItem);
ctx.CurrentItem.csr_OpenApp = "word";
ctx.currentItem_ShowHoverPanelCallback = Srch.U.getShowHoverPanelCallback(itemId, hoverId, hoverUrl);
ctx.currentItem_HideHoverPanelCallback = Srch.U.getHideHoverPanelCallback();
```

Problems solved, right? At this point the search is fixed but PDFs
don't open from document libraries in the browser. That's where
the Office Web Apps Update comes in to play!

PDF Handling with Office Web Apps Server Public Update (March 2013) using a Hybrid Approach

There was a cumulative and public update released in early March 2013 that adds additional support for PDFs in SharePoint 2013 using Office Web Apps server. The update adds a new application type named WordPDF. It allows PDFs to be opened from document libraries in the browser using the Word App Viewer.

What about search? For search, there is no change. You either need to copy the PDF Result Type and configure it to use the Word Item or modify the search display templates. (Same options as above).

However, I have come up with a hybrid approach that provides a consistent preview using the Word App Viewer but also provides the rendering of PDFs in the browser through Adobe with the search term pass-through!

Fire up SharePoint Designer 2013 and Open the Search Center Site

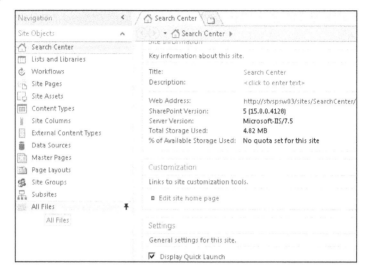

Click on All Files from the left-hand navigation

If you attempt to get the files from the Master Pages, you will not see any items once you get to the Display Templates folders.

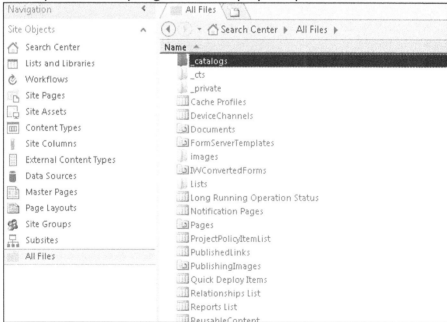

You see the list of all files in the main window.

Double-click on the _catalogs folder in the main window

This action displays the _catalogs structure under the left-hand navigation.

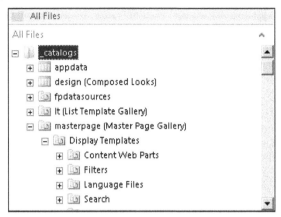

Expand the _catalogs folder, then the masterpage folder, and then the Display Templates folder.

Click on the Search folder under Display Templates

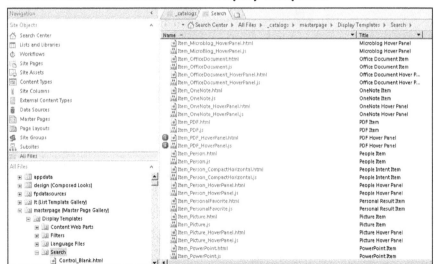

Find Item_PDF.html. Right-click and select Copy:

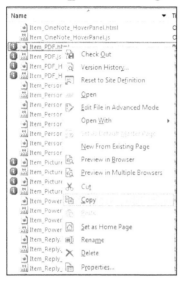

Right-click again and select Paste:

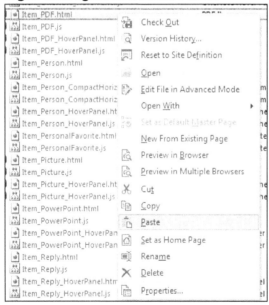

This process creates a copy of the file which appears at the bottom of the list. Find the copy and rename to something different (such as Item_PDFCustom.html):

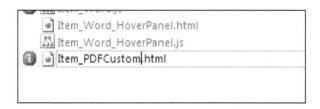

Right-click the new file and select Edit File in Advanced Mode:

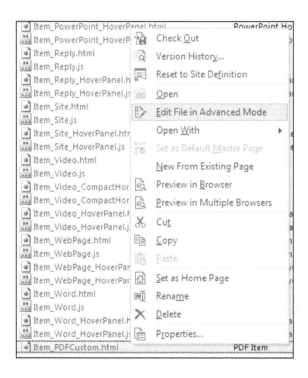

Rename the title:

```
<html xmlns:mso="urn:schemas-microsoft-com:office:offi
<head>
<title>PDF Customized Item</title>

<!--[if gte mso 9]><xml>
<mso:CustomDocumentProperties>
<mso:TemplateHidden msdt:dt="string">0</mso:TemplateHi
<mso:MasterPageDescription msdt:dt="string">Displays a
<mso:ContentTypeId msdt:dt="string">0x0101002039C03B61
<mso:TargetControlType msdt:dt="string">;#SearchResult
<mso:HtmlDesignAssociated msdt:dt="string">1</mso:Html
<mso:ManagedPropertyMapping msdt:dt="string">&#39;Titl
<mso:HtmlDesignConversionSucceeded msdt:dt="string">Tr
<mso:HtmlDesignStatusAndPreview msdt:dt="string">http:
</mso:CustomDocumentProperties>
</xml><![endif]-->
</head>
```

Change the hoverURL:

```
<body>
    <div id="Item PDF">
<!--#
        if(!isNull(ctx.CurrentItem) && !isNull(ctx.ClientControl)){
            var id = ctx.ClientControl.get_nextUniqueId();
            var itemId = id + Srch.U.Ids.item;
            var hoverId = id + Srch.U.Ids.hover;
            var hoverUrl = "~sitecollection/_catalogs/masterpage/Display Templates/Search/Item_PDFCustom_HoverPanel.js";
            &setResultItem(itemId, ctx.CurrentItem);
            var k = ctx.DataProvider.get_currentQueryState().k;
            if(!Srch.U.e(k)){
                ctx.CurrentItem.csr_Path = ctx.CurrentItem.Path + "#search=" + $urlKeyValueEncode(k);
            }
            ctx.CurrentItem.csr_Icon = Srch.U.getIconUrlByFileExtension(ctx.CurrentItem);
            ctx.CurrentItem.csr_OpenApp = "word";
            ctx.currentItem_ShowHoverPanelCallback = Srch.U.getShowHoverPanelCallback(itemId, hoverId, hoverUrl);
            ctx.currentItem_HideHoverPanelCallback = Srch.U.getHideHoverPanelCallback();
```

Replace this line:

ctx.CurrentItem.csr_OpenControl = "PdfFile.OpenDocuments";

With this one:

ctx.CurrentItem.csr_OpenApp = "word";

```
if(!Srch.U.e(k)){
    ctx.CurrentItem.csr_Path = ctx.CurrentItem.Path + "#search=" + $urlKeyValueEncode(k);
}
ctx.CurrentItem.csr_Icon = Srch.U.getIconUrlByFileExtension(ctx.CurrentItem);
ctx.CurrentItem.csr_OpenControl = "PdfFile.OpenDocuments";
ctx.currentItem_ShowHoverPanelCallback = Srch.U.getShowHoverPanelCallback(itemId, hoverId, hoverUrl);
ctx.currentItem_HideHoverPanelCallback = Srch.U.getHideHoverPanelCallback();
```

```
if('Srch.U.e(k)){
    ctx.CurrentItem.csr_Path = ctx.CurrentItem.Path + "&search=" + $urlKeyValueEncode(k);

}
ctx.CurrentItem.csr_Icon = Srch.U.getIconUrlByFileExtension(ctx.CurrentItem);
ctx.CurrentItem.csr_OpenApp = "word";
ctx.currentItem_ShowHoverPanelCallback = Srch.U.getShowHoverPanelCallback(itemId, hoverId, hoverUrl);
ctx.currentItem_HideHoverPanelCallback = Srch.U.getHideHoverPanelCallback();
```

Save the file.

This handles the opening of the PDF document in the browser.
Now for the preview.

Locate Item_Word_HoverPanel.html. Right-click and select copy:

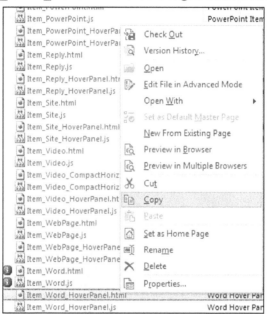

Right-click and select Paste:

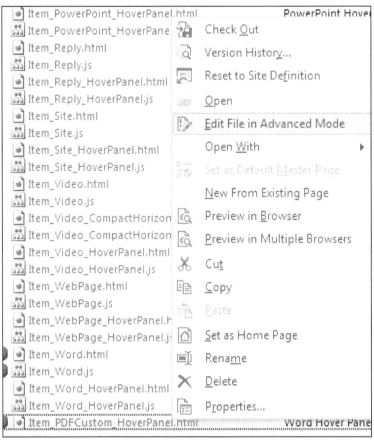

Rename the copied file (should be the same name you used for the hoverUrl value):

Right-click the new file and select Edit File in Advanced Mode:

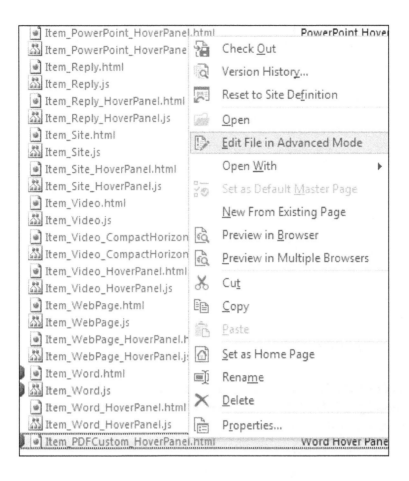

Change the title:

```
<html xmlns:mso="urn:schemas-microsoft-com:office:office" xm
<head>
<title>PDF Custom Hover Panel</title>

<!--[if gte mso 9]><xml>
<mso:CustomDocumentProperties>
<mso:TemplateHidden msdt:dt="string">0</mso:TemplateHidden>
<mso:MasterPageDescription msdt:dt="string">Displays a resul
<mso:ContentTypeId msdt:dt="string">0x0101002039C03B61C64EC4
<mso:TargetControlType msdt:dt="string">;#SearchHoverPanel;#
<mso:HtmlDesignAssociated msdt:dt="string">1</mso:HtmlDesign
<mso:ManagedPropertyMapping msdt:dt="string">&#39;Title&#39;
<mso:HtmlDesignConversionSucceeded msdt:dt="string">True</ms
<mso:HtmlDesignStatusAndPreview msdt:dt="string">http://cova
</mso:CustomDocumentProperties>
</xml><![endif]-->
</head>
<body>
```

Save the Changes.

In your Search Center, select Site Settings from the Settings menu (gear). Under Site Collection Administration, click on Search Result Types:

Site Collection Administration
Recycle bin
Search Result Sources
Search Result Types
Search Query Rules
Search Schema
Search Settings
Search Configuration Import
Search Configuration Export
Site collection features

Scroll down and find the PDF entry. Select Copy from the drop-down menu:

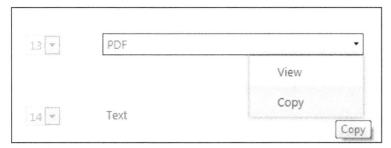

Give the type a unique name and select the PDF Customized Item as the display template:

Click Save.

Now, the search results display previews using Office Web Apps:

And the documents open in Adobe with the search term pass-through:

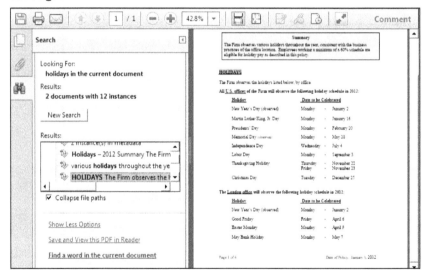

PDF Preview by Modifying Display Templates

This method of PDF previews involves the modification of search display templates. I found it better to modify the templates using SharePoint Designer 2013 although they are accessible through the SharePoint master page UI.

Fire up SharePoint Designer 2013 and Open the Search Center Site

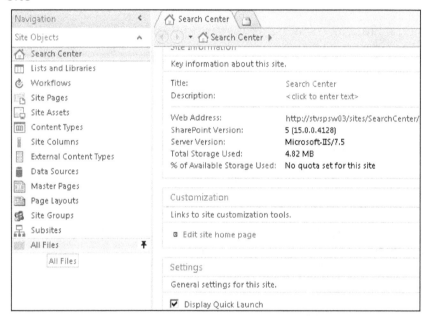

Click on All Files from the left-hand navigation

If you attempt to get the files from the Master Pages, you will not see any items once you get to the Display Templates folders.

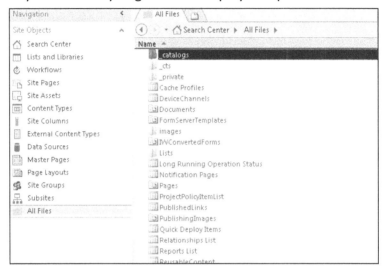

You see the list of all files in the main window.

Double-click on the _catalogs folder in the main window

This action displays the _catalogs structure under the left-hand navigation.

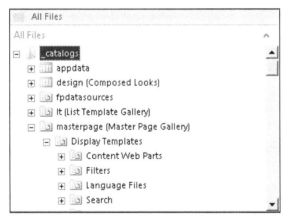

Expand the _catalogs folder, then the masterpage folder, and then the Display Templates folder.

Click on the Search folder under Display Templates

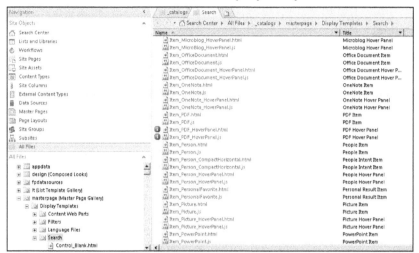

Right-click on Item_PDF_HoverPanel.html and select Edit File in Advanced Mode

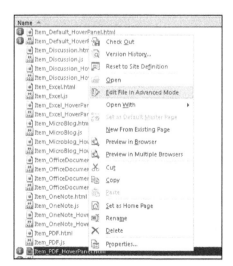

Paste the following code within the most inner <div>

```
<object data="  #= ctx.CurrentItem.Path =#  "
type="application/pdf" width="100%" height="500px" >
<p>It appears you don't have a PDF plugin for this browser/device.
You can <a href="  #= ctx.CurrentItem.Path =#  ">click here to
download the PDF file.</a></p>
</object>
```

I actually replaced the Render Header and Render Body divs with the object code.

Save the file.

When saving the file, you may get a warning about breaking from the site definition. Click OK. What happens behind the scenes is that the HTML changes are incorporated into the javascript version of the template (Item_PDF_HoverPanel.js).

Test the results. Perform a search from your search center that produces PDF document results. Hover over the PDF document to see the preview:

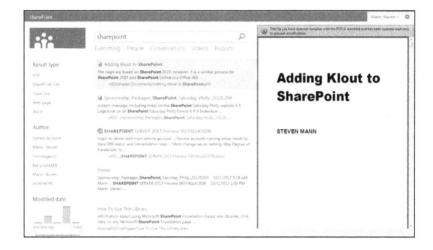

PDF Preview by Copying the Result Type (using Office Web Apps Server)

When using Office Web Apps Server with SharePoint 2013, there is an easier way to present PDF previews without having to modify the search display templates. This involves copying and modifying the PDF result type and have it render as a Word Item.

The first step is to navigate to your Search Center site settings:

Under Site Collection Administration, click on Search Result Types:

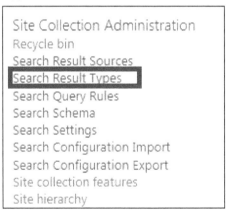

Scroll down and find the PDF entry under the Provided by the search service section. Select Copy from the drop-down menu:

On the Add Result Type page, rename the item and select Word Item under What should these results look like:

Click Save.

Run a full crawl and then perform a search that produces PDF entries. The hover preview now uses the Word App Viewer via Office Web Apps Server:

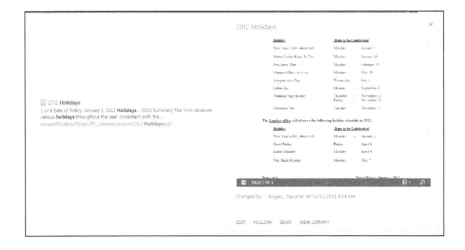

Conclusion

There are several different ways to handle the previewing of PDF search results in SharePoint 2013 by modifying the associated search display templates. The behaviors and user experience will vary depending on if you are using Office Web Apps Server 2013 or not. I hope this guide helped you understand the difference approaches and implementations that are possible.

Volume 8

How to Enhance the Search Box in SharePoint 2013

STEVEN MANN

How to Enhance the Search Box in SharePoint 2013

Trademarks

Screenshots of Microsoft Products and Services

Warning and Disclaimer

Introduction

This guide steps through the various options and settings available for the Search Box web part which allow you to enhance the user search experience in SharePoint 2013. Search Suggestions are also covered.

Stay updated with my blog posts: www.SteveTheManMann.com

Reference links and source code is available on www.stevethemanmann.com:

Adding the Verticals Drop Down to the Search Box

Before the results pages are modified, the main page of the
Search Center may be tweaked by modifying the Search Box web
part on that page.

Navigate to your Search Center:

From the Settings menu, select Edit Page:

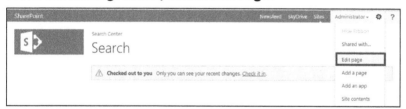

The page is presented in edit mode and is checked out to you automatically.

Click on Edit Web Part from the Search Box drop-down menu:

The Search Box Properties pane appears to the right of the page.

Select the Turn on drop-down Search Navigation option.

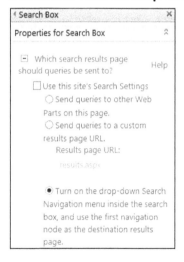

Click OK:

Check in the page:

Publish the page:

Now the user has an option to search within a defined context and navigate directly to that results page. These were previously named "scopes". Clicking Enter or clicking on the search button (magnifying glass) sends the query to the Everything page (results.aspx).

Displaying Links Next to the Search Box

You may modify the Search Box web part properties to display certain links next to the search box:

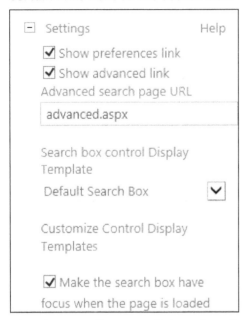

The Show preferences link option displays a link next to the Search Box where users may modify their search experience. The Show advanced link also displays a link to the right of the Search Box and navigates the user to the advanced search page.

Setting Focus on the Search Box

In the Settings section of the Search Box web part properties, there is an option to set the focus behavior:

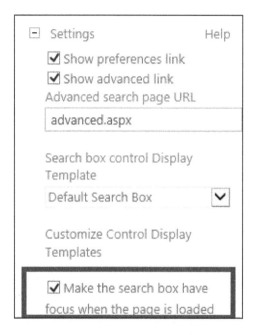

The **Make the search box have focus when the page is loaded** option places the cursor inside the search box so the user does not have to click inside to make a change.

Adding Suggestions to the Search Box

Suggestions Overview

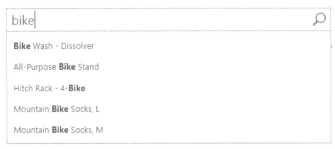

Suggestions are words or phrases that appear automatically when a user is typing search terms into a search box. Suggestions are enabled by default in both the Search Service Application and the Search Box web parts.

SharePoint automatically adds terms to the internal suggestion list based on user search actions. Once a term has been searched/queried and a result clicked a total of six (6) times, that term becomes part of the suggestion list.

This allows the suggestions to grow organically within your organization based on user past user search experiences. However, you may also add a list of suggestions to SharePoint to use. The sections to follow show you how to do just that.

When you add a list of suggestions to the Search Service Application, all previous suggestions are removed. Therefore, it is a good idea to start off with a suggestion list before going live with your new Search Center.

Create a Suggestion File

A suggestion file is just a text file that contains a word or phrase on each line. It may be anything that you feel will help your user search content. Some ideas include listing out products, clients/customers, contacts, etc. and using those values in the suggestion text file. For example purposes, I am going to list out all of the product names from the AdventureWorks sample database:

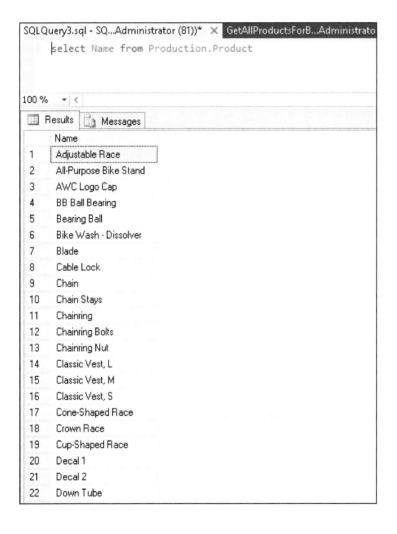

Copy and paste the list into a text file:

```
Suggestions.txt - Notepad
File   Edit   Format   View   Help
Adjustable Race
All-Purpose Bike Stand
AWC Logo Cap
BB Ball Bearing
Bearing Ball
Bike Wash - Dissolver
Blade
Cable Lock
Chain
Chain Stays
Chainring
Chainring Bolts
Chainring Nut
Classic Vest, L
Classic Vest, M
Classic Vest, S
Cone-Shaped Race
Crown Race
Cup-Shaped Race
Decal 1
Decal 2
Down Tube
External Lock Washer 1
External Lock Washer 2
External Lock Washer 3
External Lock Washer 4
External Lock Washer 5
External Lock Washer 6
External Lock Washer 7
External Lock Washer 8
External Lock Washer 9
Fender Set - Mountain
Flat Washer 1
Flat Washer 2
Flat Washer 3
Flat Washer 4
Flat Washer 5
Flat Washer 6
Flat Washer 7
```

Save the text file and get ready for import.

Import the Suggestion File

To import a suggestion file, navigate to your Search Service Application and click on Query Suggestions under the Queries and Results section of the left-hand navigation:

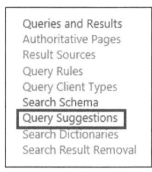

Click on the Import from text file link on the Query Suggestion Settings page:

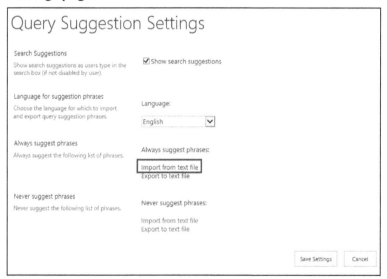

Click the Browse button to locate and select your suggestion text file:

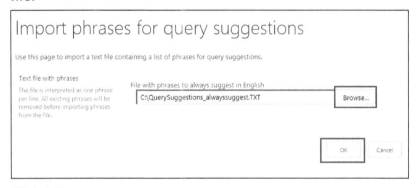

Click OK.

For good measure, click Save Settings:

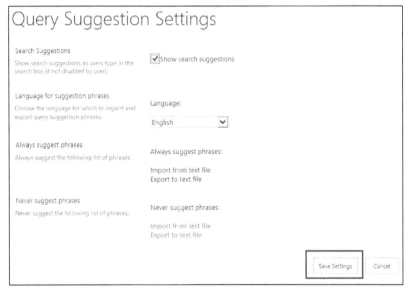

Process Query Suggestions

After the suggestions are imported, they will not appear until they are processed. They are processed via a timer job in SharePoint.

So instead of holding your breath to see the suggestions work, navigate to Central Administration and click on Monitoring from the left-hand navigation:

Click on Review job definitions under Timer Jobs:

On the Job Definitions page, scroll down to the bottom and click the arrow to go to the next page:

1-100 ▸

Scroll up on the next page and click on the Prepare Query Suggestions:

Title
My Site Instantiation Interactive Request Queue
My Site Instantiation Non-Interactive Request Queue
My Site Instantiation Non-Interactive Request Queue
My Site Second Instantiation Interactive Request Queue
My Site Second Instantiation Interactive Request Queue
Notification Timer Job c02c63c2-12d8-4ec0-b678-f05c7e00570e
Notification Timer Job c02c63c2-12d8-4ec0-b678-f05c7e00570e
Password Management
Performance Metric Provider
Persisted Navigation Term Set Synchronization
Persisted Navigation Term Set Synchronization
Prepare query suggestions
Product Version Job
Query Classification Dictionary Update for Search Application Search Service Application.
Query Logging
Rebalance crawl store partitions for Search Service Application

On the Edit Timer Job page, click Run Now:

Job Description

Prepares candidate queries for query suggestion and performs pre-computations for result block ranking.

Job Properties

This section lists the properties for this job.

Web application: N/A

Last run time: 4/19/2013 5:43 PM

Recurring Schedule

Use this section to modify the schedule specifying when the timer job will run. Daily, weekly, and monthly schedules also include a window of execution. The timer service will pick a random time within this interval to begin executing the job on each applicable server. This feature is appropriate for high-load jobs which run on multiple servers on the farm. Running this type of job on all the servers simultaneously might place an unreasonable load on the farm. To specify an exact starting time, set the beginning and ending times of the interval to the same value.

This timer job is scheduled to run:

○ Minutes   Starting every day between
○ Hourly   [1 AM ▾] [00 ▾]
◉ Daily   and no later than
○ Weekly   [11 PM ▾] [30 ▾]
○ Monthly

[Run Now]   [Disable]   [OK]   [Cancel]

The time job runs fairly quickly. You may view the results as explained in the next section.

View Suggestion Results

Navigate to your Search Center and type in a few letters that match some of your suggestion words/phrases:

The matching suggestions appear under the Search Box. You may modify the suggestion behavior as explained in the next section.

Configuring Suggestions in the Search Box Web Part

By default the Search Box is set to show suggestions. You may also elect to show people name suggestions. This provides functionality similar to an auto-complete. You may configure how many suggestions appear and how long it takes to show suggestions based on the number of minimum characters configured.

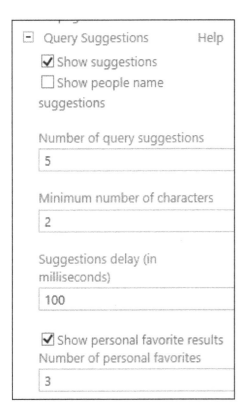

The Search Box web part on each results page in your Search Center may be modified to change the behavior of suggestions and thus modify the user experience.

I like changing the minimum characters to 1 and the suggestions delay to 50 milliseconds. This allows the suggestions to appear quicker.

Volume 9

Synonyms and Sugar in SharePoint 2013 Search

STEVEN MANN

Synonyms and Sugar in SharePoint 2013 Search

Copyright © 2013 by Steven Mann

Trademarks

Screenshots of Microsoft Products and Services

Warning and Disclaimer

Introduction

This guide discusses the use of the search thesaurus, spelling words, and suggestions in SharePoint 2013 Search.

Stay updated with my blog posts: www.SteveTheManMann.com

Reference links and source code is available on www.stevethemanmann.com:

Adding a Thesaurus for Synonym Results

Synonyms Overview

When people search for items, they may use familiar terms or acronyms accordingly. However, the content may have terms spelled out or contain similar words as the search term but not the same word.

For example, if I search for "Philadelphia" but some content uses "Philly", I won't see those results. Similarly, if I search for "GE" but some content uses "General Electric", I won't see those results either.

This is where synonyms come into play. You may generate and upload a thesaurus file that contains pairs of terms such that when the first term is searched, the second term is also searched.

Create a Thesaurus File

A thesaurus file is a comma separated file which contains three columns: Key, Synonym, and Language. The Language column is optional and therefore your file technically could only contain pairs of synonyms.

An example of thesaurus file contents is as follows:

Key,Synonym,Language

IE,Internet Explorer

Internet Explorer,IE

HR, Human Resources

Human Resources, HR

Notice there is no "vice-versa" implied and therefore for each pair you may want to include the opposite order. Think of it as "when I search for this", "also include this".

To create a thesaurus file, simply open a text editor, add the header, and then go to town adding pairs of synonyms:

```
synonyms.txt - Notepad

File  Edit  Format  View  Help
Key,Synonym,Language
IE,Internet Explorer
Internet Explorer,IE
HR,Human Resources
Human Resources,HR
Philadelphia,Philly
Philly, Philadelphia
Bicycle,Bike
Bike,Bicycle
```

Save the file as a .csv file.

Import a Thesaurus File

In order to import your thesaurus file, you need to use PowerShell.

Launch the SharePoint 2013 Management Console and enter the following two command lines (using your own path for the -FileName parameter):

$ssa= Get-SPEnterpriseSearchServiceApplication

Import-SPEnterpriseSearchThesaurus -SearchApplication $ssa -Filename
\\sp2013srv\c$\ThesaurusFile.csv

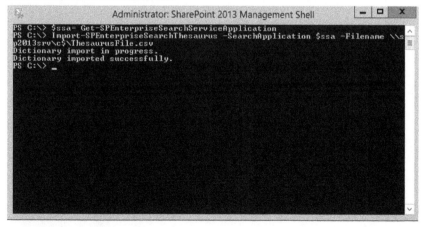

The thesaurus file is imported.

Test Synonyms in Search

To test the thesaurus file, simply search for various synonyms that the file contains. I knew with my example external data, that "Bike" was used often but "Bicycle" was not. I included these synonyms in my thesaurus file. Now when I search for Bicycle, I retrieve results that include Bike:

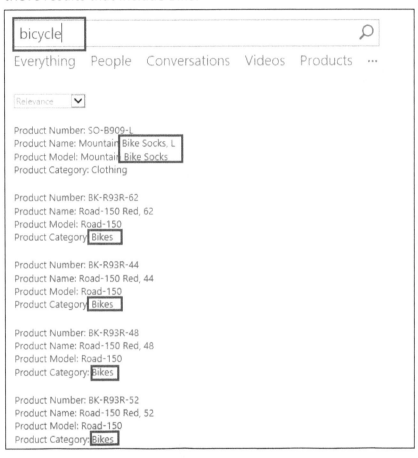

Adding Spelling Words

When looking to summarize the use of spelling words and show examples of the Did You Mean? functionality in SharePoint 2013 Search, I realized that Microsoft MVP, Waldek Mastykarz, already had this topic well summarized on his blog (http://blog.mastykarz.nl). Therefore, with his permission, I have adapted content from his blog post "SharePoint 2013 Query Spelling Inclusions for the masses" to complete this section.

SharePoint 2013 Search provides you with the query spelling suggestion capability that suggest correcting spelling mistakes in search queries. By default this capability is configured to automatically build the spelling suggestions dictionary. By changing the configuration settings it is possible to manually maintain the query spelling suggestions dictionary.

Spelling Words Overview

One of the biggest investments in SharePoint 2013 was the integration of the enterprise-class search engine, previously known as FAST, with the SharePoint Search engine. As a result SharePoint 2013 Search offers us top of the class search capabilities.

Among all the different search-related capabilities of SharePoint 2013 Search are query spelling suggestions – also known as 'did you mean'. Whenever you enter a search query, SharePoint 2013 Search will check if all words have been spelled correctly and if not, it will suggest the correct spelling.

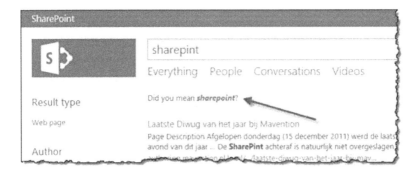

And while the query spelling suggestions do work by default, there are some challenges to how they are configured.

Query Spelling Suggestions

SharePoint 2013 Search knows two types of query spelling suggestion dictionaries: a dynamic and a static one. The dynamic dictionary is maintained by SharePoint itself based on the content in the search index, while the static one is maintained by yourself. Out of the box SharePoint uses the dynamic query spelling suggestions dictionary.

For a term to become a part of the dynamic query spelling dictionary, it has to occur in at least 50 documents. The interesting part is however the content alignment process which is used by the dynamic dictionary and which is enabled by default. This process is triggered when the term that occurs the most in the search index has been found in the preconfigured number of documents (1000 by default; can be changed using PowerShell) and then the dictionary is built.

If you are interested in exploring the default configuration of query spelling suggestions you can use the following PowerShell snippet:

$ssa = Get-SPEnterpriseSearchServiceApplication

Get-SPEnterpriseSearchQuerySpellingCorrection -SearchApplication $ssa

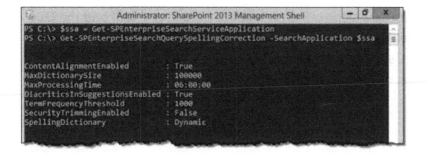

What if, however, you don't want to rely on the standard process of building query spelling suggestions dictionary and want to build and maintain one yourself? The next sub-section explains how to add or remove your own words from SharePoint 2013 Search.

Adding Spelling Words to Your Search Service

Adding spelling words to your search service first involves switching the spelling dictionary mode to static, and then adding spelling words into the spelling term sets. This sub-section explains both of these processes.

SharePoint 2013 uses two Global Term Sets called **Query Spelling Exclusions** and **Query Spelling Inclusions** to define the query spelling suggestions. Both Term Sets are ignored in the dynamic mode however, so before you can start entering your own suggestions, you have to switch to the static dictionary.

To switch to the static query spelling suggestions dictionary you have to run the following PowerShell snippet:

$ssa = Get-SPEnterpriseSearchServiceApplication

Set-SPEnterpriseSearchQuerySpellingCorrection -SearchApplication $ssa -SpellingDictionary

This will change the query spelling suggestions dictionary mode to static and with this SharePoint 2013 Search will start using your values stored in the two Term Sets.

Configuring query spelling suggestions is easy and comes down to creating new Terms under the **Query Spelling Exclusions** Term Set (for words which you never want to have suggested) and the **Query Spelling Inclusions** Term Set (for words which SharePoint should suggest). There are a few rules when it comes to configuring query spelling suggestions:

1. a query spelling suggestion is a single word, so **SharePoint** is a correct suggestion but **Sharing Points** is not

2. when creating query spelling suggestions only the first level of Terms is taken into account. SharePoint 2013 Search expects a list of words that it can then use to detect spelling mistakes. Query spelling suggestions Terms are in no way a dictionary such as **SharePint > SharePoint**, where the Term **SharePoint** would be a child Term of **SharePint** denoting in a way that every time SharePoint 2013 Search stumbles upon **SharePint** in a search query it should suggest **SharePoint** instead. This part is done by SharePoint automatically without our help.

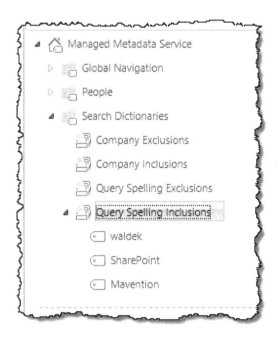

Processing Spelling Words

After you have entered your query spelling suggestions Terms, they won't appear directly in the search results however. Instead you have to wait for the **Search Custom Dictionaries Update** Timer Job to run or execute it manually yourself.

After the job has executed and the query spelling suggestions from the static dictionary have been processed they will be used in SharePoint search results.

Adding Suggestions to the Search Box

Suggestions Overview

Suggestions are words or phrases that appear automatically when a user is typing search terms into a search box. Suggestions are enabled by default in both the Search Service Application and the Search Box web parts.

SharePoint automatically adds terms to the internal suggestion list based on user search actions. Once a term has been searched/queried and a result clicked a total of six (6) times, that term becomes part of the suggestion list.

This allows the suggestions to grow organically within your organization based on user past user search experiences. However, you may also add a list of suggestions to SharePoint to use. The sections to follow show you how to do just that.

When you add a list of suggestions to the Search Service Application, all previous suggestions are removed. Therefore, it is a good idea to start off with a suggestion list before going live with your new Search Center.

Create a Suggestion File

A suggestion file is just a text file that contains a word or phrase on each line. It may be anything that you feel will help your user search content. Some ideas include listing out products, clients/customers, contacts, etc. and using those values in the suggestion text file. For example purposes, I am going to list out all of the product names from the AdventureWorks sample database:

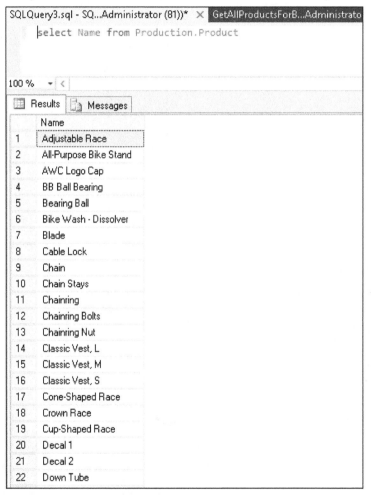

Copy and paste the list into a text file:

```
Suggestions.txt - Notepad
File  Edit  Format  View  Help
Adjustable Race
All-Purpose Bike Stand
AWC Logo Cap
BB Ball Bearing
Bearing Ball
Bike Wash - Dissolver
Blade
Cable Lock
Chain
Chain Stays
Chainring
Chainring Bolts
Chainring Nut
Classic Vest, L
Classic Vest, M
Classic Vest, S
Cone-Shaped Race
Crown Race
Cup-Shaped Race
Decal 1
Decal 2
Down Tube
External Lock Washer 1
External Lock Washer 2
External Lock Washer 3
External Lock Washer 4
External Lock Washer 5
External Lock Washer 6
External Lock Washer 7
External Lock Washer 8
External Lock Washer 9
Fender Set - Mountain
Flat Washer 1
Flat Washer 2
Flat Washer 3
Flat Washer 4
Flat Washer 5
Flat Washer 6
Flat Washer 7
```

Save the text file and get ready for import.

Import the Suggestion File

To import a suggestion file, navigate to your Search Service Application and click on Query Suggestions under the Queries and Results section of the left-hand navigation:

Click on the Import from text file link on the Query Suggestion Settings page:

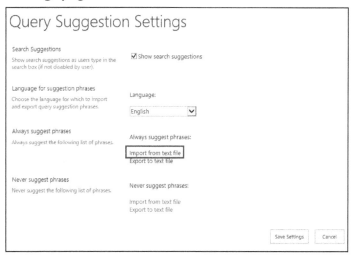

Click the Browse button to locate and select your suggestion text file:

Click OK.

For good measure, click Save Settings:

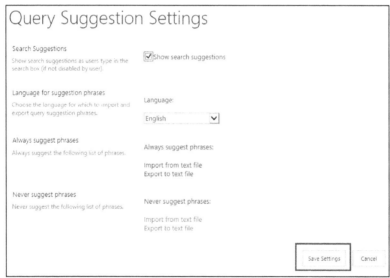

Process Query Suggestions

After the suggestions are imported, they will not appear until they are processed. They are processed via a timer job in SharePoint.

So instead of holding your breath to see the suggestions work, navigate to Central Administration and click on Monitoring from the left-hand navigation:

Click on Review job definitions under Timer Jobs:

On the Job Definitions page, scroll down to the bottom and click the arrow to go to the next page:

1-100 ▸

Scroll up on the next page and click on the Prepare Query Suggestions:

Title

My Site Instantiation Interactive Request Queue

My Site Instantiation Non-Interactive Request Queue

My Site Instantiation Non-Interactive Request Queue

My Site Second Instantiation Interactive Request Queue

My Site Second Instantiation Interactive Request Queue

Notification Timer Job c02c63c2-12d8-4ec0-b678-f05c7e00570e

Notification Timer Job c02c63c2-12d8-4ec0-b678-f05c7e00570e

Password Management

Performance Metric Provider

Persisted Navigation Term Set Synchronization

Persisted Navigation Term Set Synchronization

Prepare query suggestions

Product Version Job

Query Classification Dictionary Update for Search Application Search Service Application.

Query Logging

Rebalance crawl store partitions for Search Service Application

On the Edit Timer Job page, click Run Now:

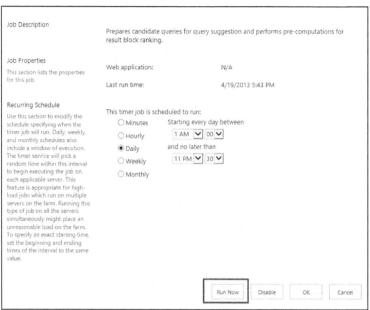

The time job runs fairly quickly. You may view the results as explained in the next section.

View Suggestion Results

Navigate to your Search Center and type in a few letters that match some of your suggestion words/phrases:

The matching suggestions appear under the Search Box. You may modify the suggestion behavior as explained in the next section.

Configuring Suggestions in the Search Box Web Part

By default the Search Box is set to show suggestions. You may also elect to show people name suggestions. This provides functionality similar to an auto-complete. You may configure how many suggestions appear and how long it takes to show suggestions based on the number of minimum characters configured.

The Search Box web part on each results page in your Search Center may be modified to change the behavior of suggestions and thus modify the user experience.

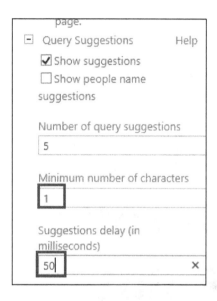

I like changing the minimum characters to 1 and the suggestions delay to 50 milliseconds. This allows the suggestions to appear quicker.

Volume 10

Enhancing Image and Picture Results in SharePoint 2013 Search

STEVEN MANN

Enhancing Image and Picture Results in SharePoint 2013

Trademarks

Screenshots of Microsoft Products and Services

Warning and Disclaimer

Introduction

This guide walks through the configuration and behaviors of image/picture search results. Without any modifications to your search center and search service application, the crawling and presentation of image/picture items may not always be consistent.

Stay updated with my blog posts: www.SteveTheManMann.com

Reference links and source code is available on www.stevethemanmann.com:

Previewing of Images Not Stored in Picture Libraries

When images are stored in "regular" document libraries such as Site Assets, they are uploaded as documents. When the library is crawled, the results are the actual list item and not the image itself. Even if you add the Image or Picture content type to the library and modify the item, the result is still treated like a list item. The reason the images are coming back as items is because image file types such as .jpg and .gif are not in the list of the search file types. To correct this, follow the steps in this section.

Launch Central Admin:

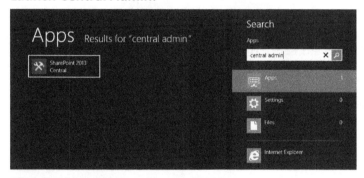

Click on Manage service applications:

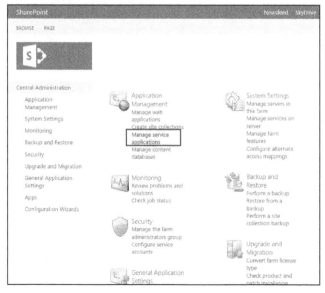

Click on Search Service Application:

On the left hand side click on File Types:

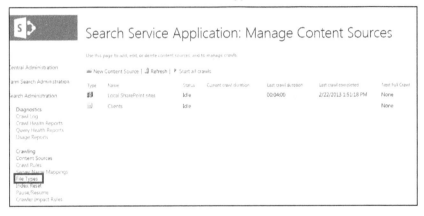

On the File Types page, click on New File Type:

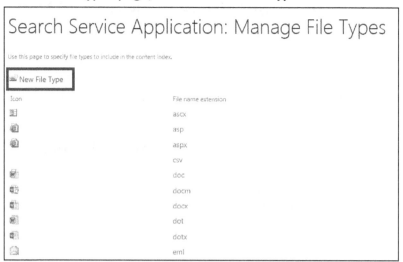

Enter an image file type such as jpg and click ok:

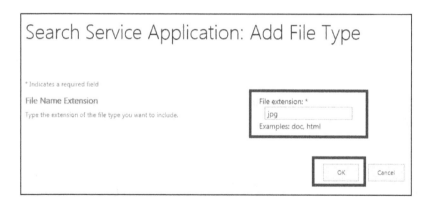

Repeat the process for other gif, png, tif, etc. or any other image types you want to handle.

Run a full crawl.

After the crawl is completed, the search results of the images should appear as their filename instead of a list item.

Previewing of Images Stored In Picture Libraries

After going through the steps in the previous section, it turns out even images stored in Picture Libraries are returned as files themselves. The hover works fine but you should be able to take advantage of the image result type. This section corrects that issue.

In your Search Center site collection select Site settings from the settings menu:

Under Site Collection Administration, click on Search Result Types:

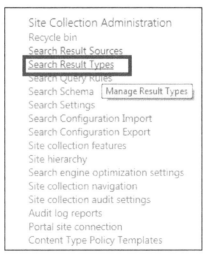

Scroll down and find Image. Use the drop-down menu and select Copy:

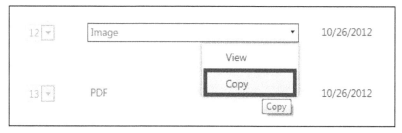

On the Add Result Type page, select Picture Item under What should these results look like?

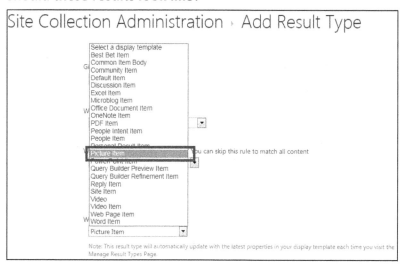

Click Save:

Run a search for an item in a Picture Library:

There is a preview image right in the results! That's great but that didn't happen in image results from other types of libraries - on to the next section.

Consistent UX for Images Results

After performing the steps in the previous sections, the results from a Picture Library and non-Picture Library look different. It is not consistent for the user:

You may correct this by editing the Picture Item display template (Item_Picture.html).

Fire up SharePoint Designer 2013 and Open the Search Center Site

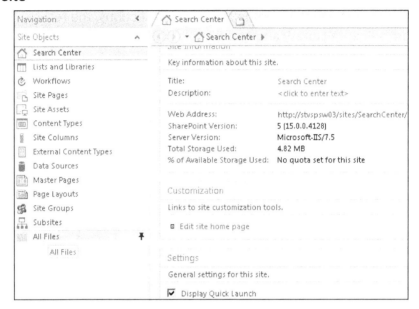

Click on All Files from the left-hand navigation

If you attempt to get the files from the Master Pages, you will not see any items once you get to the Display Templates folders.

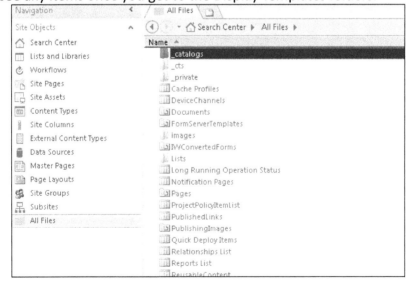

You see the list of all files in the main window.

Double-click on the _catalogs folder in the main window

This action displays the _catalogs structure under the left-hand navigation.

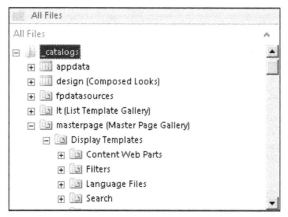

Expand the _catalogs folder, then the masterpage folder, and then the Display Templates folder.

Click on the Search folder under Display Templates

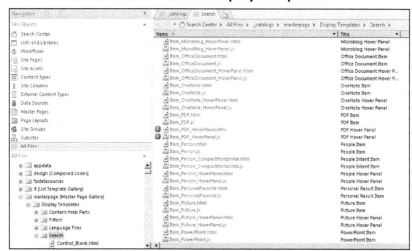

Locate the Item_Picture.html file, right click, and select Edit in Advanced Mode.

Simply add an else statement to the if in the middle of the code:

```
else {
ctx.CurrentItem.csr_PreviewImage = ctx.CurrentItem.Path;
}
```

Save the file and run a search again:

desert OR penguins

Everything   People   Conversations   Videos

Penguins Picture
Penguins.jpg ... SiteAssets/**Penguins**.jpg
stvspsw13/SiteAssets/**Penguins**.jpg

Desert
Desert.jpg ... Pic Lib/**Desert**.jpg
stvspsw13/Pic Lib/**Desert**.jpg

Now all images that are returned have a preview image in the results!!!!

Displaying a Preview Image in the Image Search Result Hover Panel

Hovering over the image search results does not show a larger preview image:

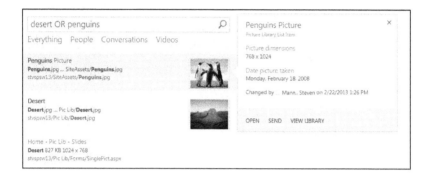

Modify the Item_Picture_HoverPanel.html file and add the following code right before the first if statement:

```
<div class="ms-srch-hover-imageContainer">
<img id=" #= ctx.CurrentItem.csr_id =# " src=" #= $urlHtmlEn-
code(ctx.CurrentItem.Path) =# " onload="this.style.display='block';" />
</div>
```

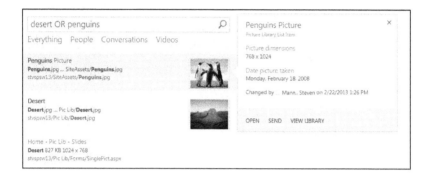

Save the file and refresh the search results. A larger image shows in the hover now:

Displaying Image Results Horizontally (with Hover)

SharePoint 2013 contains templates to display both videos and people in a horizontal fashion presenting a nice presentation in the Everything search results. For an example of the Video horizontal display see the previous chapter.

It would be nice to also have this horizontal functionality for images as well as display the hover panel on the items (since the people and video horizontal displays do not incorporate the hover panel out-of-the-box).

Launch SharePoint Designer 2013 and navigate to the search center display templates (similar to the steps outlined in Appendix A).

Locate the Item_Picture.html, right-click and select Copy:

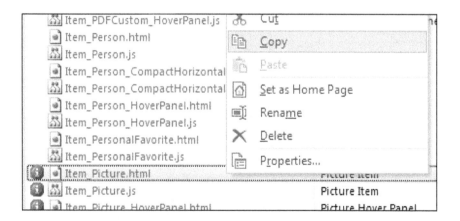

Right-click again and select Paste:

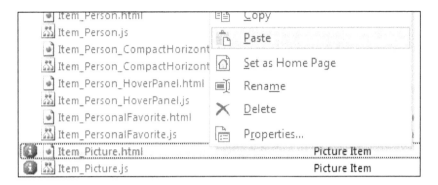

Rename the copied file to Item_Picture_CompactHorizontal:

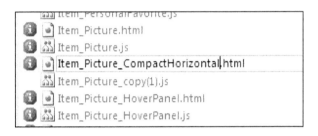

Right-click again and select Edit File in Advanced Mode:

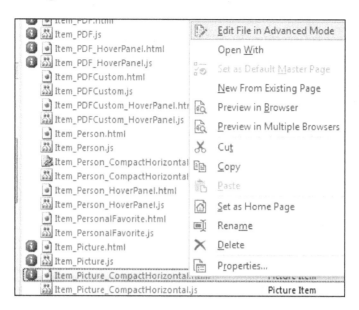

Rename the title and the main div id:

```
<html xmlns:mso="urn:schemas-microsoft-com:office:office" xmlns:msdt="u
<head>
<title>Picture Horizontal</title>

<!--[if gte mso 9]><xml>
<mso:CustomDocumentProperties>
<mso:TemplateHidden msdt:dt="string">0</mso:TemplateHidden>
<mso:MasterPageDescription msdt:dt="string">Displays a result tailored
<mso:ContentTypeId msdt:dt="string">0x0101002039C03B61C64EC4A04F5361F38
<mso:TargetControlType msdt:dt="string">;#SearchResults;#</mso:TargetC
<mso:HtmlDesignAssociated msdt:dt="string">1</mso:HtmlDesignAssociated>
<mso:ManagedPropertyMapping msdt:dt="string">&#39;Title&#39;;:&#39;Titl
<mso:HtmlDesignStatusAndPreview msdt:dt="string">http://covspwf01/site
<mso:HtmlDesignConversionSucceeded msdt:dt="string">True</mso:HtmlDesi
</mso:CustomDocumentProperties>
</xml><![endif]-->
</head>
<body>
    <div id="Item_Picture_CompactHorizontal">
<!--#
        if(!$isNull(ctx.CurrentItem) && !$isNull(ctx.ClientControl)){
            var id = ctx.ClientControl.get_nextUniqueId();
            var itemId = id + Srch.U.Ids.item;
            var hoverId = id + Srch.U.Ids.hover;
```

Add the following code as shown in the image below:

```
<!--#
if (!Srch.U.n(ctx.CurrentItem.ParentTableReference) &&
ctx.CurrentItem.ParentTableReference.TotalRows > 1) {
 #-->
```

```
<!--#
} else {
 #-->
```

Scroll to the bottom and add an additional closing bracket:

```
_#-->
                    _#=ctx.RenderBody(ctx)=#_
                    <div id="_#= $htmlEncode(hoverId) =#_"
        </div>
<!--#_
            [   }   ]
        }

_#-->
        </div>
</body>
</html>
```

Between the if and the else that you pasted first, enter the following code as shown in the image below:

```
<div id=" #= $htmlEncode(itemId) =# " name="Item" class="ms-srch-people-
intentItem" onmouseover=" #= ctx.currentItem_ShowHoverPanelCallback =# "
onmouseout=" #= ctx.currentItem_HideHoverPanelCallback =# ">
<div id="ImageInfo">
<!--#
var pathEncoded = $urlHtmlEncode(ctx.CurrentItem.Path);
var encodedName = $htmlEncode(ctx.CurrentItem.Title);
 #-->

<ul id="ImageCard">
<li id="ImagePic">
<a clicktype="Result" href=" #= pathEncoded =# " title=" #= encodedName =# ">
<img id="PicPreview" src=" #= pathEncoded =# " height="80px" width="80px"/>
</a>
</li>
<li id="ImageTitle">
<div id="imageTitle" class="ms-textSmall ms-srch-ellipsis" title=" #= encodedName
=# "> #= encodedName =#  </div>
</li>
</ul>
<div id=" #= $htmlEncode(hoverId) =# " class="ms-srch-hover-
outerContainer"></div>
</div>
</div>
```

```
<!--#_
        if (!Srch.U.n(ctx.CurrentItem.ParentTableReference) && ctx.CurrentItem.ParentTableReference.TotalRows
_#-->
        <div id="_#= $htmlEncode(itemId) =#_" name="Item" class="ms-srch-people-intentItem" onmouseover="_#= ctx.
            <div id="ImageInfo">
<!--#_
                var pathEncoded = $urlHtmlEncode(ctx.CurrentItem.Path);
                var encodedName = $htmlEncode(ctx.CurrentItem.Title);
_#-->
            <ul id="ImageCard">
                <li id="ImagePic">
                    <a clicktype="Result" href="_#= pathEncoded =#_" title="_#= encodedName =#_">
                        <img id="PicPreview" src="_#= pathEncoded =#_" height="80px" width="80px"/>
                    </a>
                </li>
                <li id="ImageTitle">
                    <div id="imageTitle" class="ms-textSmall ms-srch-ellipsis" title="_#= encodedName =#_">
                </li>
            </ul>
            <div id="_#= $htmlEncode(hoverId) =#_" class="ms-srch-hover-outerContainer"></div>
        </div>
    </div>
<!--#_
        } else {
```

Save the changes and then navigate to your Search Center.

From your Search Center site settings, select Search Query Rules from the Site Collection Administration section:

Site Collection Administration
Recycle bin
Search Result Sources
Search Result Types
Search Query Rules
Search Schema
Search Settings
Search Configuration Import
Search Configuration Export
Site collection features

Select the Local SharePoint Results (System):

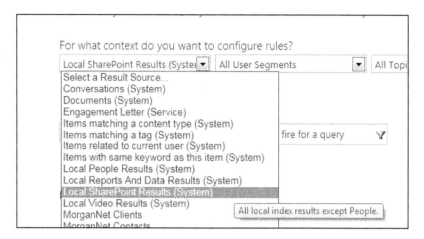

After the Query Rules load on the page, scroll down and find the Image entry. From the drop-down menu select Copy:

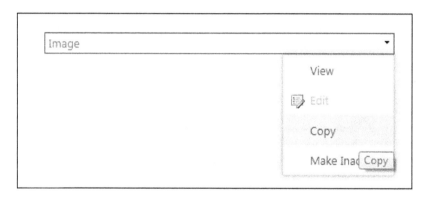

Change the Rule name:

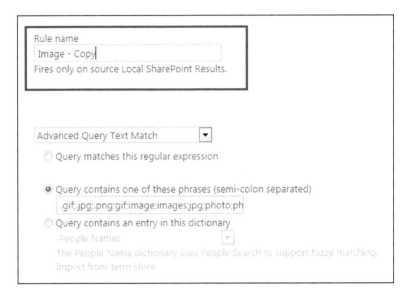

Scroll down to the Actions sections and click on edit to edit the result block:

Actions

When your rule fires, it can enhance search results in three ways. It can add promoted results above the ranked results. It can also add blocks of additional results. Like normal results, these blocks can be promoted to always appear above ranked results or ranked so they only appear if highly relevant. Finally, the rule can change ranked results, such as tuning their ordering.

Promoted Results

Add Promoted Result

Result Blocks

    Promoted (shown above ranked results in this order)
        Images for "{subjectTerms}" edit remove

Add Result Block

Change ranked results by changing the query

Change the Query. (I was not getting expected results from the InternalFileType property. Therefore I changed my query filter to "(ContentType:PictureItem OR ContentType:Image)").

I also changed the amount of items to 6:

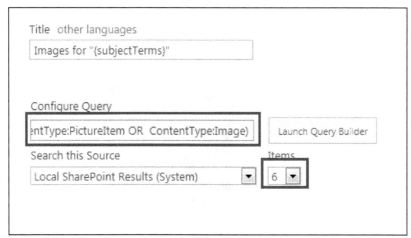

In the Settings select This block is always shown above core re-sults and also change the Item Display Template to the new Pic-ture Horizontal template:

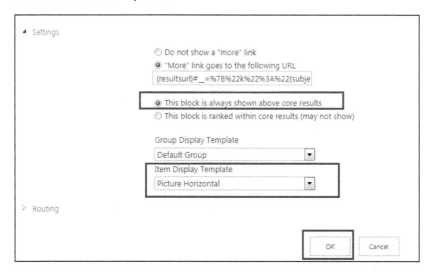

Click OK. Click Save on the Edit Query Rule page.

Navigate to your search page and peform a search for images:

Images for "computer"

04-05-07_1016.jpg   04-05-07_1017.jpg   04-05-07_1018.jpg   04-05-07_1423.jpg   04-05-07_1424.jpg   04-05-07_1425.jpg

SHOW MORE
About 408 results

The images display horizontally and the hover works as well:

computer image

Everything   People

Relevance ▼

Images for "computer"

04-05-07_1016.jpg   04-05-07_1017.jpg

SHOW MORE
About 408 results

04-05-07_1017.jpg   ×
Picture Library List Item

Picture dimensions
480 x 640

Changed by

OPEN   SEND   VIEW LIBRARY

www.ingramcontent.com/pod-product-compliance
Lightning Source LLC
Chambersburg PA
CBHW071420050326
40689CB00010B/1912